Ode to Ageless Love

A Selection of Rhyming Poems

Ode to Ageless Love

A Selection of Rhyming Poems

Freeman J. Wong

Bestview Scholars Publishing

Published in 2025 by:

Bestview Scholars Publishing Ltd.

48 Leafield Dr., Unit B., Toronto, ON M1W 2T2 Canada

Email: bestviewscholars@gmail.com Website: **www.bestviewscholars.com**

ISBN: 978-1-896848-33-4 ISBN (epub): 978-1-896848-34-1

Cover design: Jeffrey Huang

Library and Archives Canada Cataloguing in Publication

Title: Ode to ageless love : a selection of rhyming poems / Freeman J. Wong.
Names: Wong, Freeman J., 1956- author
Identifiers: Canadiana (print) 20250290278 | Canadiana (ebook) 20250290286 | ISBN 9781896848334
(softcover) | ISBN 9781896848341 (EPUB)
Subjects: LCSH: Love—Poetry. | LCGFT: Poetry.
Classification: LCC PS8595.O596 O34 2025 | DDC C811/.6—dc23

This poetry book is adapted from nine of the author's published stories. The family guidelines and "Farewell to Sons" in "A Shining Father," first appearing in *The Beautiful and the Absurd: Stories for Our Times,* were edited for iambic improvement. Several double-vowel words may have been weighed as single or double syllables by AI and other counters, yet as two only by certain readers. Here, their measure rests on how the line is spoken aloud. In a perfect world, the author would wish for five flawless iambs in every line, and two perfect rhymes to bind each couplet, but imperfections exist through these pages. Some rhymes fall true in American English but falter in British, and others the reverse. Colloquial and archaic words appear by design, each carrying its own purpose. Also, whenever the choice arose between the eye and the ear, the ear prevailed.

This is an original print edition of *Ode to Ageless Love: A Selection of Rhyming Poems.*

Contents

Ode to Ageless Love

This tale of youth, now forty winters worn,
Shall cloak your name like dawn in misty morn.
Sunshine, both flame and grace your spirit shows,
A blush of strength that time still kindles glows.

Dear Sunshine, youth's sweet wine, how bright it poured!
There one heart's bruise became love's swift reward.
In your hometown, by fate's divine command,
We met, two souls touched by God's guiding hand.

The Institute's great halls, where voices rose,
Became the field that granted my repose.
Old losses melted in your glance's glow;
I walked the row that grace ordained to grow.

Then fortune grinned: two joys in one bright glance;
Your Flora shone where Yale had pined by chance.
Let thanks be carved where Cupid's arrows fell;
Your hand linked theirs and rang sweet love's twin bell.

Their golden vows with silver threads now twine;
Two couples forged by fate's eternal design.

Oh, Tricapital's double-storied grace:
One trip, two hearts, four lives bound in one place!

Embraced by hope, I blessed the skies above;
For who but God could grant my perfect love?
That instant spark, though clichés call it trite,
Was fate's own hand that fused us at first sight.

No strangers then; your gaze knew all my seams,
Read every thought, and swam through all my dreams.
You lit my hope, you armed my timid heart,
Made kings of dust, and courage from each part.

Your smile like dawn! Your laugh like wind-chimes' song!
Each knowing glance that proves where I belong.
For you I'd toil, for you I'd dare the grave;
Such courage springs when souls find whom they crave.

We spoke first words and shared a stirring start,
Then deeper, thrilling talks where heart met heart.
Your fourth-year spring released a dazzling dart:
Two kindred souls, one love, one work of art.

I knew my worth: a man who'd love you true;
You knew your grace: a wife in virtue's view.
Together sworn, a pair the stars admire,
My dreams took flight, set by your spirit's fire!

That "Hello" sparked what years could not erase:
From chatter, to deep talk, to love's bold face.
In sweet spring air, two hearts threw off disguise;
No need for oaths, we saw it in our eyes.

You'd be my rock, and I would be your light;
Two golden souls forged flawless in love's sight.
Let others watch, let tongues gape, let them fade;
Our hearts'd be one though kingdoms fell and laid.

You breathed new life through me, my soul unfurled:
I felt her smile had, Lord, remade the world.
My sweet dreams soared past where the sky turns black,
No moon too dim, no sun too bright to track.

Did you know this? Perhaps the truth was hid;
How could I speak what heart and conscience bid?
So soon, so fast, would any maid believe
Such ardent vows that dawn before they weave?

No shame I own, just youth's unbridled fire,
A young man's heart, a young man's right desire.
When love is true, it cannot help but pour;
It spills, it shines, it aches to give you more.

No girl before had stirred this joy so deep;
My first love rests in sacred trust I keep.

All that I was, all that I could e'er be,
Would bloom for you for all the world to see.

That Afternoon

That afternoon, we met your school nearby,
Inside my hotel room, two hearts, both shy.
We sat upon the bed, hands clasped so tight,
Lost in our words, in joy, in love's new light.

Then angry knocks destroyed our fragile peace,
A threat of law, a storm that would not cease.
No time to pause, they'd break it down, I knew,
Or drag us off in shame, our names untrue.

To answer slow meant dire disgrace and blame:
"Prostitution," that vile, defiling name.
What'd be "too slow"? A breath, a gasp, a shoe
Half-donned in haste sufficed to damn us through.

But Heaven smiled: we sat clothed, pure, upright,
Though flushed with youth and trembling at their might.
They scanned your face, then mine with judging eyes,
Checked papers cold, then left like loathsome flies.

That gasp of air when loud boots turned to go,
Still soiled our joy and stained love's afterglow.

Oh, Sunshine, think! Had lust, not love, held sway,
Then hells of shame would be our endless pay!

You, still a student, while I, teacher sworn,
A model sought, would be snubbed, left forlorn.
We'd be paraded, drowned in jabs and scorn,
Our names in leaflets, all our honor torn!

Then when you bade me meet your parents' sight,
Though Goat Town scorned, I knew your heart was right.
They gave consent, yet laced with doubt's alloy,
For love like ours defied their world's employ.

Now years prove clear what needless fear denied:
That Yale and I wore honor as our bride.
No men more true, more steadfast could they find,
Though judgment's ghost once nipped so close behind.

I grudge not: parents guard their gems by right,
Though in the process lenses lose their light.
Tricapital days were so bright, so brief;
Then Goat Town's arms enclosed my heart's belief.

No happier sun had warmed my life's cold air,
No soul so light, no love so ripe, so rare!
Proud past all sound, my found, my flawless prize,
I floated through each day, star-struck, star-wise.

Your face gleamed near in all I shaped or planned,
Yet work grew fiercer, honed by love's firm hand.
What fools might call distraction proved untrue;
For love, like sun, lent strength to all I knew.

I laughed alone—what sight that must have been,
Yet every cell hummed bright with joy unseen.
My stride grew bold, my shoulders squared with might,
My chin held high, my gaze drank in the light.

A newfound force rushed through my veins and bones,
So kind to students, friends, and strangers' tones.
Love's magic spell had shaped my world anew,
And all who crossed my path felt kindness too.

Each dawn I sought my Yale, that steadfast friend,
To queue where steam and rice-paste rolls ascend.
While waiting there, we'd trade our tender news
Of Flora's laugh, your wit, your bright reviews.

Those talks at dawn, so brief yet golden-lit,
Were honeyed sparks to light the long day's wit.

We dreamed the months until you'd southward tread,
To don white gowns, to vow, to share our bread.

Once, soft, you teased, half-jest, half-sweet decree,
"I'll heed your word on work, but let me see!"

I swore it wasn't pride, nor whims unkind,
But life's hard ledger left no choice behind.

Both Yale and I, with degrees clasped in hand,
Held posts to shield a wife from want's demand.
Yet jobs for you were scarcer, fierce to chase,
Two posts in one bright city, harder place!

Tricapital, though grand, turned cold, austere:
Dear tongues like yours it could choose not to hear.
You smiled, no grudge, no tempest in your voice,
"I fret not, love; I trust you, I rejoice."

Such faith! Such grace! Though steep, our path was clear,
And every step drew home and Heaven near.
The brightest spark that set my heart aflame:
Your letters came, each word your gentle claim.

I'd write back bravely, even though unskilled,
Yet every line with truth and longing filled.
Then joy! You came, your father at your side,
To Goat Town where love couldn't be denied.

How deep my thanks for steps so bold, so true;
For days so sweet, hearts turning one from two.
Your visit proved our bond was strong and real,
Your father's presence like a silent seal.

With classes paused, we stole what time allowed
By quiet ponds, in shadows soft and proud.
We clung, we kissed, as all fierce lovers would,
Though chaperoned by kinship's watchful good.

Yet wonder came: though guarding virtue's gate,
He e'en let us embark, to tempt our fate.
One night, one rural path, one starry air,
Such trust, such grace, 'twas just too rare to bear.

That Night

A night no time could steal, no mind erase:
Not yours, not mine, not even time's own trace.
That night you curled within my trembling hold;
Two souls, one fire, one story yet untold.

We'd booked two rooms, though one was all we sought;
They came, checked papers, and left joy distraught.
Oh, Tricapital's ghosts! Must they pursue,
As if love's pulse were something foul to view?

We burned, we ached, no shame in that pure need,
No guilt for how our racing hearts would plead.
Young, fierce, and free, what right had they to bind
The sacred pull of body, will, and mind?

The hotel stood, a plain and creaking frame;
No gates to guard, no locks to curb our flame.
You feared the dark; I feared far darker schemes
That hands might harm you mid your fragile dreams.

Then, joy, your door sighed open, soft, unsure,
And there you stood, my solace, and my cure.
I'd left my latch unbarred, you slipped inside;
You were scared, so I said, "Now here abide."

We lay clothed, close, yet trembling, half-untamed,
For laws like knives above our passions aimed.
Not fear for me, but love's own shield I raised;
One reckless night, and futures could be razed.

Your whisper came: "Should we not claim our right?"
God! How I burned, yet choked back Heaven's light.
"If we dare now," I groaned, "come dawn's harsh stare,
We may not walk free past the courthouse square."

No state seal pressed where our true vows were sworn,
Just smirking clerks who judged our love with scorn.
Those Tricapital ghosts, those prowling eyes,
All state-made snares for "sinners" they despise.

Yet there we clung, one bed, one breath, one ache;
A pure fire, yet bound for some cold law's sake.
Let others whisper, clutch their brittle law;
We wore our hunger without pause or flaw.

But caught unclothed? Disgrace would strike like steel;
"Corrupting youth," a charge no plea could heal.
Days jailed, my name dragged through the grime of scorn,
While you, left lost, our fledgling love outworn.

Your father guarded my home all alone;
No phones to call, his presence went unknown.
If dawn found us in chains, what would he eat?
What streets would guide his weary, stranded feet?

One night's delight could torch all we had planned:
No work for me, no bridge to reach your land.
Those rigid years! Their chains both tight and cold,
Yet shielding you outweighed the fire on hold.

So through the dark we clung, but not as one,
Our bodies dressed, our battle left undone.
I watched the door, each shadow, each faint sound,
Not fearing law, we broke no sacred ground.

You trembled still, I wove my arms a claim:
She feared the night, yet solace bore no shame.

No knock returned, the stars crept past the pane;
At dawn we rose, half-grieved, yet safe again.

Oh, what a might-have-been! Had we but dared,
No storm had come, no blade our joy had bared.
Yet life, you tease, we'd never truly know
What risk was real, what phantom made us slow.

A lifetime's question lingers in my chest:
What thought of me did your hushed heart attest?
Was pride or wounded scorn your mind's unrest:
A man who froze where bolder men progressed?

If you saw wisdom in my tempered hand,
I'd kneel to thank you for that grace unplanned.
If scorn had touched your gaze, I'd bear the weight;
For true love must choose when risk outweighs fate.

Yet past that night, I turned to warrens grim:
The bureaucrat's maze, cold and stark and dim.
To bring you south, each thread I dared to trace
Through Goat Town's gates, that walled and watchful place.

Twice-bound my school, by state and province, held
The chains that clipped your flight, your dreams repelled.
And she, that matron of my spurned embrace,
Sat crowned where all files met her face-to-face.

Could spite eclipse her stamp? I feared, yet knew:
No petty power would part me e'er from you.
Through back roads, through the blaze of frontal war,
I'd win you home, to me, to Goat Town's shore.

Then came bright news: a friend who knew the maze,
Though not the throne, could soften stern pathways.
No beggar I! My work stood tall, unmarred;
For you, I'd learn new trades, though fierce or hard.

A teacher's gown? I'd fold it like a veil
To don a salesman's suit or trader's tale.
Goat Town, elsewhere, or past the ocean's crest,
Where'er you bloomed would be our rightful nest.

No wealth you sought, just hands to build, to hold,
And love would spin our straw to harvest's gold.
Oh, love's fierce might! Oh, hope's unyielding flame!
Each day apart burned slow, yet stoked the same.

That Moment

A moment etched where time could not corrode,
Not yours, not mine, nor mem'ry's heavy load.
That night withheld, yet dawn would soon repay
The wait, the want, the debts of longing's day.

Then word! My friend brought news to light the air:
Flora's last test meant that you, too, bloomed there.
Your books all closed, your student's yoke undone;
The race was won, our waiting's end begun!

That year stretched vast, each hour a year's own girth,
Yet aching nights still sang your priceless worth.
A visit first, your train or mine to bear
Two bodies home, two souls past parting's snare.

I sprinted to the phone, heart wild, unkept,
"You've crossed the line! Goat Town should you accept.
Not yet for good, we know those old slow gears,
But come, my love, for tight hugs free of fears."

This time, we'd meet unchained by threat or law;
No knocks would haunt our door, no clutching claw.
We'd wed, we'd build home, hear a child's first cry,
And paint our days with sun, not stranger's eye.

But life, not art, deals wounds no script would dare;
Your voice cut through: "Can't join you, to be fair."
"Is this the end?" I gasped. Your "Yes" struck deep,
A blade no plea could dull, no prayer could keep.

The thunder roared! My mind went white, went still;
No past, no words, no will to climb that hill.
What fled that hour? What vows tore loose, unspun?
I woke to ash where love had burned, had won!

The world's bright king now slumped, a hollow shell;
Red molten iron changed to cold dull bell.
Just this remains: my stumble, numb, unwise,
To gasp to Yale: "My girl has cut all ties."

You, fully grown; you, pledged, then left me torn,
My first, my only sun, my rose, my thorn.
All dreams I sowed lay trampled where they fell;
Your choice was made, I had to wish you well.

No recall guards how breath or pulse prevailed,
Just voids where love once bloomed, then wrecked, then failed.
A gaping void where mem'ry should abide,
No ghost of grief, no shade of days that died.

What cruel jest! We'd pored on tales so trite,
Then lived our own—love's merciless dark night.
How swift the arc: first glance, first bed, first vow,
Then one stark "No" to sever every bough.

When sense returned, I wore misfortune's hand,
Yet cast no stone upon your parting stand.
Though brief our dance, its light still warms my pains:
Gold hours no fate could taint, no theft profanes.

I hoard each laugh, each glance, each whispered beam,
Not as they were, but as they'd gleam in dream.

I write to fix what time might blur or shade:
Not love's first fire, but how its embers fade.

When forty years have silvered all our care,
We'll speak of *why* love burns, not *how* we dare.
I sipped its sweets, then gagged on bitter breeze,
A rose late-bloomed in winter's killing freeze.

Your blow struck numb, yet shock tore clear my sight:
This was my karmic debt, my judgment rite.
For girls who waited, hearts I failed to see,
Sweet souls let down, all due to one blind bee.

And those I craved? My roots too poor, too plain,
My mother's need oft deemed loss, not love's gain.
Still others shone, good homes, good souls, good light,
Yet I refused, with reasons thin or trite.

I realized, when you left, the scales were true:
All hurts I'd dealt came back to pierce me through.
Yet grief, my sage, has tutored me to own
Not just the ache, but seeds that love had sown.

Your choice left ruins where my wild heart stood,
Yet since you found your joy, I called it good.
But love, once spilled, will flood in strange designs;
It tinted worlds and drew uncanny signs.

Now mind iced still, heart stalled, and blood ran cold,
A hollow man where warmth had brimmed of old.
Then, pained and drained, I heard your late reprieve,
But time had forged new bonds I couldn't leave.

Another saw your castoff, bruised yet new,
And dared to claim what you'd withdrawn from view.
Strange balm it was, in love's abandoned keep,
To find her faith could stir my roots from sleep!

I warmed to one whose sight pierced through my blight:
No kin's crude taunts, no ledger's shallow fight.
She took the ash your fire had left behind,
And blew one ember back to living mind.

How strange! Those girls who feared my mother's weight
Would chain their lives, now laugh at fate's debate.
She spurns my walls and streets her soul denies;
As hens flee hawks, she pines for open skies.

When Goat Town held her for the newborn's cry,
She wept until we freed her homeward sigh.
Then Toronto's towers? More tears, more pleas,
She missed her fields, she missed her root-bound ease.

The city's chill, the country's soft, warm earth,
Two worlds apart, yet each knew equal worth.

What brides had dreaded never came to pass:
No yoke, no clash, just love through separate glass.

My vow was newly pledged when you called last,
No flame left then to reignite the past.
A good soul held my honor in her hand,
No second spark could break that steadfast band.

Where once my blood ran fierce as forge's light,
Now ice had crept to still the pulse of might.
No embers left to fan, no bridge to build,
Just two lives stalled, with hollows never filled.

Two flawed vows sworn beneath indifferent skies,
Yet in our hearts, the ghost of love still sighs.
First love still calls when newer loves grow cold,
When nights turn long, and silent tears are rolled.

Four decades on, our bond still softly gleams,
Not threads unspooled, but gold in woven dreams.
Your daughter soars, I hear her triumphs true,
My own, like yours, have forged their paths anew.

I feel that man who once adored your face,
Till mirrors shout: Time paints its brutal trace!
Gray strands, thin skin, these inkblots wisdom sends,
True feelings stay where marriage oft pretends.

Love greens the soul, though vows may rust and strain,
And you, my north star often flick with pain.
You prove luck clings to those who hold one name
To whisper when the dark crowds in like flame.

That Email

That email burns where all else fades to gray;
Not yours, not mine could quite erase its sway.
Your life veiled still, my own in shadows cast,
Four decades' tale, yet this brief, stumbling past.

Then Montreal, a stranger typed your name,
A ghost, a scam? I froze at love's old game.
He was ignored till I knew who and what:
Your voice, your words, "a cloud he'd once forgot."

Forgot? My pulse roared back: *Could've been my life!*
No sky could hold such clouds in fleeting strife.
Then phones rang clear, two men bound by your glow,
While time stood still, and old events breathed flow.

I let him bridge the silence, wide, untrod;
Next dawn, your words! My breath, my pulse, my god!
Your daughter shone, your vows stood firm, yet near:
"I miss you still." The past rushed back so clear.

We should have been one flesh, one hearth, one flame,
But fate, that thief, tore love to blame and shame.
No lid contains such embers—lawless, due;
Regret's no crime when love's the ghost we rue.

One lifetime's weight: that choice we left unmade,
One shadow clasped where'er our souls parade.
When treasures vanish, longing becomes blessed;
Where love burned brightest, absence scars the chest.

No spouse should chain what time cannot erase;
Let grief breathe free, or stir a fiercer blaze.
To grudge such tears but feeds the hungry flame;
To trust may spare the heart its costly shame.

For love's true measure lies in bold desire,
And unvoiced embers never lose their fire.
For childless hearts, the door stands wide, unsealed;
A pen's swift stroke, and all is past, repealed.

But parents? Chains of gold their vows enforce;
For young eyes starved of love pay love's divorce.
"No self, no worth," the wound their silence fights,
While we, masked tight, perform our borrowed heights.

Yet greatness lurks where mothers, fathers play,
Though love's torch dims to guide the fledgling's way.

Your single dove could flee the withered bough;
My brood, all fine, still claim my hollow vow.

We paint joy's lie where cracks run deep and green,
Not for our sake, but to fill space unseen.
Your name flashed bright, my heart leapt, then sank low,
To learn your joy's cracks only love's lens show.

If only sighs dissolve where timelines twist,
No key to rewrite fate's clenched, stubborn fist.
Then hackers stole what time had spared so long;
Our thread snapped clean, the dark absolved of song.

Four decades since that first electric glance,
I scour the void for one lost breath of chance.
If ghosts of emails drift where you now tread,
Send but one line, let *Yahoo!* raise the dead.

That Conversation

Yet still the sun, unswayed by loss or prayer,
Paints dawn to dusk the same relentless glare.
Our dates, untouched by rust or rot, abide;
No yesterday, just *now*, they take our side.

You bend to tasks, and lo! Your youth has fled;
I faced on last birthday the oath I'd pled.

Unanswered here, I'll seek beyond the veil,
This love's last riddle where no stars grow pale.

The New Year's sun had scarcely dried its dew,
When fate spun bright, a thread I dared pursue.
My inbox blinked: Singdoe's kind voice appeared;
Good news received, and lo, my heart upreared.

I cheered her wins, then, trembling, penned the plea:
"Help find this friend of class of '83?"
No star seems dead while embers clutch one spark;
Her keystrokes there may pierce the endless dark.

Dawn struck and shocked! Your digits, clear and new,
More gold than fortune's wildest dream could strew!
My hands shook lightning; clocks crawled, slow, unkind,
Till sunset lent its hour to bridge the mind.

Three times I called, three silences, three walls,
While iPhones mocked love's fragile, fenceless halls.
I'll seek tomorrow's landline, plain and dear;
'Twill breach the void where wires refuse to cheer.

Twelve hours apart, I watched the creeping light,
Then plowed through snow that stalled love's long stalled flight.
The clock struck ten past ten in your world's peek;
'Twas late for most, but you were mine to seek.

One ring, two rings, then silence, vast, unfurled,
Till *"Sunshine!"* cracked the four decades' ice swirled.
Your voice dissolved my bones to spring's first dew,
While time, that thief, stood slack-jawed, frowned in blue

You probed my low, hoarse voice with tender care;
I lied 'twas winter chill, but truth laid bare.
'Twas sleepless nights, heartsick, hope's fever fed;
For forty years this question burned unsaid.

"Sunshine, should laughter drown us, or tears fall?
Where does one start when lifetimes crowd our hall?"
Words weighed like stones, yet light as dust in air,
A past too vast for any tongue to dare.

"Why severed us that day, forty years flown?"
You shrieked in shock, "The axe was yours alone!"
My joy dissolved, now trembling, now afraid,
Two truths at war where once our hearts had stayed.

Some shadow crossed what time could not defend,
Some blade unseen had sliced love's golden end.
No hand unbloodied, no tale without pains:
Just ghosts that weep what might have been the chains.

No answer came, now stood I, self-accused,
While justice pled this wound stay unrefused.
"Recall your voice, cold words of that phone call:
'I won't come south. It's over. That is all.'"

You fired back I had hometown girl stood near,
A shadow shared each time you begged my ear!
By Heaven's light, I had no third hand kept:
Three charges flung, and all three false you wept.

No other face could steal my gaze from thee,
No phantom girl, no hometown's harsh decree.
You were my sun, my only moonlit sphere;
No rival shade could haunt our golden year.

"And is your wife not proof?" you charged anew.
But trust my oath, as God knows what is true!
If guilt were mine, I'd kneel and bare each sin,
But slander stains where love has ever been.

The timeline stands: our bond first torn apart,
Then night school's chance refilled my hollow heart.
No go-between, and no hometown's design,
Just Goat Town's neighbor, slow to mend what's mine.

"So near, yet far," you mused. My riposte burned:
Your "no" left ghosts; some men have hanged or turned.
I chose ink, not a noose, to mourn my due,
Yet forty years still ache to question you.

That night we nearly wed, what seaside place?
You named it; moonlight carved lines in my face.

How strange—the mind, when grief strikes like a knife,
Seals whole years off to dull the ache of life.

I thought you'd found some brighter star, I sighed,
And bowed to love though half my soul had died.
Before the phone, in silence, stunned I stood,
A ghost who lost both name and sense of good.

"Had we that night unleashed what fire demands,
Might threads have knotted tight as wedding bands?"
You paused, "Or snarled our paths with thornier twine,
A debt no 'if' or 'but' could then unwind."

I feared the same, I feared guilt's cruel hand;
It quenched the fire no tide could e'er withstand.
Two hearts, one proof: real love's equation known,
Some locks stay fixed lest greater grief be sown.

You grumbled how those distant bus rides drained:
No calls, just ink, while love's frail threads remained.
You never swore to sever us—your claim.
Then whose voice broke us? Whose hand snuffed the flame?

"Oh, life!" I howled. "Must time's joke play a ghoul?
A fool's script penned where lovers dream and drool!"
Two truths now fight where one sweet past had been,
While clocks laugh loud at what they could have seen.

A garage sale trinket, marked down, half-priced,
Some fine son shone where my rough roots sufficed.
I brought no throne, just hick's grit, mother's need,
Faults stacked like bricks where your proud kin took heed.

Aware they probed my past, my gut ran cold;
'Tis now clear that the script their verdict told!
No country boy could clear those gilded gates,
Where love's pure coin weighs less than bloodline's rates.

That spurned girl's mother, throned where power kills,
Held Goat Town's gates with bureaucratic drills.
Her inked stamp ruled who crossed the city's line,
While love, unbound, scoffed at her frail design.

No oath I swore to trade my heart for gold,
No state could cage what freeborn souls uphold.
Let files turn dust, their ash won't stain our flight;
True love scorns gates that bureaucrats bolt tight.

No shock their spite would deal a heavy blow,
But still it hurt like fresh wounds burned in snow.
That loathed girl's kin could smear my name with ink,
But love scorns cages forged by clerks' small think.

Let lecterns rot, I'd trade this threadbare gown
For merchant's gold to lift your anchor-town.
Fivefold the wage! No state leash bound my hand;
We'd build our ark where they could wreck no land.

All cards I dealt you, every feud, each scar;
But now, raw truth's smears part us from afar.
Yet time, not faults, undid what love had planned:
You, still my crown; I, king of might-have-land.

"My father swore he'd snap my bones in twain!"
You flung the words like stones against my brain.
"Why silence then?" I choked, yet no reply,
Just open wounds beneath the hollow sky.

You sighed you were a lost girl, "princess" bred;
You had no spoon that stirred, no guest you fed.
What care had I for feasts or flawless hands?
Life's craft we'd learn—pots, pans—where love demands.

"Your hometown men rule hard," you then believed;
Now time unmasks what shadows worked, I grieved.
'Twas rivals, false friends, kin's conniving art,
Or her I'd left, who struck with poisoned dart.

No single blade, but needle-stings compound
To drain love's cup before its real taste found.
Now blame's old feast turns ash upon the tongue;
Time stole the gold, then left the ledger hung.

Love's darkest tales? A rival slain, or lies
That rot reputes till star-crossed love complies.
Such plagues persist, no shore, no age immune,
Yet we? Just pawns in some deranged typhoon.

You mused I played your guide; I laughed, appalled,
"A bumbling scout whose life was tripped and stalled!"
You still claimed 'twas my hand that led your way
To life that carved the soul you have today.

No bitterness, just gold those moments cast,
Each laugh, each step, each 'us' that could not last.
You spoke of streets we'd walked, of skies we'd known,
While decades' dust still swirled where seeds were sown.

No verdict sealed, no ledger's final line,
Just ghosts of answers, faint as summer wine.
The mystery breathes, but softer now—less stark:
Some loves are solved by how they leave their mark.

No guilt confessed, yet no more storms to wage,
Just laughter's truce on time's long-tattered page.
Your charges stood, half-answered, half-denied,
But forty years have bleached their venom's pride.

Work still unknown, but clocks tolled midnight's moon;
We paused, then sealed the past with one last boon:
"Was this talk worth the scars it carved so deep?"
"Like silver reels," you sighed, "where shadows weep."

"Then fade to black," I murmured, "credits scroll;
Our last frame lingers, searing soul to soul."
Through storms of years, through lies and time's harsh grasp;

We stand at last where all our trials now clasp.

Reunion

Now logic bowed, we raced to that same shore,
Where youth once paused, now ripe to claim its store.
No cloth, no fear, no clock's tight leash denied,
Just waves that sighed what decades couldn't hide.

Oh, love struck gold! Two bodies, one bright spark,
As if the years had burned to mere remark.
That beach, those sheets, now scripted to atone;
Not forty lost, but forty years new-grown.

Or, gilded suites where silks, not sand, were spread;
We clung, yet clothed, one heart, one soul, one bed.
No flesh unveiled, but truer vows took flight;
Love's highest art: to want, yet choose the light.

Oh, love unstained! Two flames no lust could bend,
Where holding hands outshone what bodies rend.
Let readers pick which close our script defers:
Each crowns the truth, our love scorns any stirs.

All threads were spun by Heaven's hidden hand,
Each knot, each fray part of our life preplanned.
No flawless vows, perfection's curse would flee
Where love's too bright for mortal bonds to see.

Yet here we stand, though late, still clasped, still true,
Two weathered scripts life's stage has breathed anew.
Does this reunion outshine common vows?
Enough to kneel, not question, at the *how*'s.

So raise the curtain! Let our last act start:
Not man and wife, but souls no world could part.

Lover's Rescue

Rayhan left Bridle Mall with roses twined,
In glossy wrap, by plastic sheen well lined.
He sniffed their scent and blew a kiss so dear,
As though to Lilly, held his heartbeat near.

He took swift strides toward the new Finch Road:
"This bus won't do! You see that big full load!"
Next bus preferred, but lunch at half ere twelve
Forced him aboard; no pause for dreams to shelve.

He jumped in, though 'twas packed from wall to wall;
No seat remained, he stood through rise and fall.
He clutched the blooms, breathed deep their Lilly-scent;
He smiled, lost in the joy they would present.

The bus lurched forth, then raced at speed uncurbed,
Till brakes screamed hard—the man's balance disturbed.
He nearly crashed, but saved his blooms instead,
Then stood, pants fallen, heat of shame ahead.

"Oh God!" the girl beside him screamed aloud;
All eyes turned toward him within the crowd.

They saw him standing there in underpants;
His trousers pooled around his shoes 'mongst rants.

Face reddening, he yanked them up with speed;
A wary woman warned him to take heed.
She grabbed her cellphone, readied it to call.
"My belt has broken!" Rayhan begged of all.

Thus she stepped closer, verified the claim:
The buckle had detached, 'twas not the same!
The nosy passenger now laughed outright,
Put phone away while pondering the sight.

To fix the belt with flowers in one hand
And pants in other, he appeared well-planned.
Stems thrust beneath his armpit for firm hold,
Then shoulder dropped, pants pinned tight 'gainst his fold.

Both hands thus freed, he tried the strap's repair,
But missing pin defeated his despair.
He tried without the buckle: 'twas too short;
Cool sweat beaded and streamed in salty port.

Lilly will understand, he told his heart;
Her parents' judgment fed his fear's sharp dart.
Would they accept a boy of lesser means?
Or would their banker world reject poor teens?

His choices slim, Rayhan stuffed belt in hold,
Then bent to loosen right shoe's knotted fold.
He pulled the lace, unsure if 'twould prevail:
"Strong save two flimsy points, worn-out and frail."

Through belt loops slipped, he drew the lace up tight;
Thank God! It beat the belt that failed in blight!
The strangers' eyes beamed joy at job well done;
This lad's quick-witted grace had brightly won.

Now pants secured, he rose, both eyes alight,
The bus exploded in applause's might.
"Unreal!" he breathed, amazed at fortune's shift,
A shoelace triumphed where fine new belts drift.

At Rose-and-Rose on Bloor, Rayhan arrived,
His cell displayed eleven, time derived.
The hostess led to Room Three, private, grand,
Where Lilly waited, art-absorbed, so spanned.

She wore new elegance, in thoughtful gaze,
At painting's pair engaged in love's strange maze.
Back turned, she missed his entry through the door,
So Rayhan planned a game to cheer her more.

"Surprise!" he charged, hands blindfolding her sight,
"Now roses here, sweetheart, for your delight!"

"Hands off me now!" she shrieked in fierce reply,
Removing his tight hold with frantic cry.

Shocked by rejection, once fond touch allowed,
Her thrashing broke his shoelace, pants unplowed.
Through open door, gaped diners at the scene:
Pantless man clutching woman, harsh and keen.

Screams filled the air; phones flashed for pictures' sake,
As restroom-suited man rushed to partake.
He dashed and tore Rayhan from Lilly's frame,
To quell the chaos and wreck passion's flame.

"You?!" snorted she, her hot red anger steamed;
"Oh God! Do pardon me!" Rayhan's fear screamed.
He yanked his pants, tied lace with broken strand,
Wished earth would swallow where he dared not stand.

This wasn't Lilly! Dread began to creep;
No guess required, truth plunged dark and deep.
He'd booked this room for lunch with parents dear,
Yet they arrived, and Lilly not appear.

Her mother scanned his jacket, shoes, and hair,
His missing lace, a sight beyond compare.
With icy glare that pierced his soul's confine,
She stripped his worth, each flaw drawn line by line.

"Where's Lilly?" Flushed, he stammered out distress;
Her mouth's twist answered coldly, wordless press.
She rose, her exit final as a knell,
Left Rayhan stranded in rejection's cell.

In three swift minutes, cops burst through the door,
Asked for ID, posed questions three or more.
"You're charged with sexual assault!" they cried,
Then seized his trembling hands and had them tied.

Then Lilly rushed in, late, to Room Three's frame,
Met Rayhan cuffed, her world aflame with shame.
The whole restaurant stared, aghast and grim,
At this young man led off on suspect's whim.

"Rayhan! What happened? Why?" He heard her plea.
"Call lawyer now!" he begged, seeing life debris.
She dialed quick; soon counsel stood beside,
At station where no dreadful truths could hide.

In fright she asked if he had fought a fight.
Rayhan told all: belt's snap, the flowered sight.
Mistook her mother too, but did not know!
Cops laughed at the lace tale, yet charged the blow.

Remained in question, freedom's path though clear:
Withdraw the charge, or court would hold him near.

Next day he'd face the judge's stern decree:
Case dropped or trial for the world to see.

While lawyers parleyed, Lilly called her kin;
Rayhan prayed, "God, keep my job, let me win!"
One hour missed and he'd be fired that same date;
Or trial's stain would seal his future fate.

Reputation ruined, work gone, love lost,
Each would result in a horrendous frost.
Lilly knew Mother held the crucial key;
"This honest man would touch no one but me!"

She rushed back home, her mission sharp and keen,
"Mom, 'tis just grave misunderstanding's scene.
Rayhan's belt snapped, he used a shoelace belt,
Which broke when joy in him was 'bout to melt.

"He mistook you for dear me from behind;
The lace snapped, pants fell, showing an absent find.
He'd never harm, nor strip with intent base,
So spare this good man trial's shameful chase!"

Discharge by mother could free him today,
But you may expect what she would relay.
"Reconsider this bond you claim to hold,
Before his fate my verdict will unfold."

"Mom, I know you seek best for my life's gift,
But Rayhan's just a friend: no pledge, no lift.
We're testing waters, nothing firm or deep,
So far, no promise made, no vow to reap.

"I'll choose no man without your yes and Dad's,
So fear not meetings: just brief, friendly ads."
Her sobs still wet, yet logic clear and straight,
She pled for mercy, sealing Rayhan's fate.

Her mother sighed, revealing a soft face,
"I'm pleased you grasp my stance in time and space.
I trust your choice in partners will be wise,
But hugging half-undressed draws shrieking cries.

"A woman'd call police, not only me;
Such public acts would even make men flee."
"Of course," said Lilly, "it's no joy but sore.
Since Rayhan's just a friend, we'll meet no more.

"No rush to know him, should you both approve,
Then, and just then shall I make my next move."
"Truly?" Her mother warmed, now free from dread.
"As good as gold." Assurance gently spread.

They hugged, but Lilly whispered, soft and clear,
"Trial for his mistakes would cause me fear."

Even a stranger's plight would weigh one's soul.
"I'll free him now!" Mom's mercy took control.

She called the cops, withdrew the charge with speed,
"Cheer up, my child!" Her mercy met the need.
Lilly smiled through wet thanks, with tears impearled,
While Rayhan walked free into his saved world.

She waited, sans consent, where freed men walked,
Rayhan released, no charge, no record talked.
The incident sealed tight from public view,
Known just to cops, kin, lawyer—very few.

She whispered strategy into his ear,
How love would bloom past parents' fret and fear.
He nodded, kissed, left station's stark domain,
Now 5 p.m., fatigue a leaden chain.

He trudged toward the mall's west-facing light,
Appeared before buffet's new, lavish sight:
"Lunch: All you eat—$15!" proclaimed,
Well-dressed crowds queued, their comfort famed.

I'll feast for freedom! Thought began to soar
When distant chaos crashed through joy's restore.
At lot's east edge, four thugs forced driver's brawl;
Rayhan saw justice twist to lawless fall.

Twelve thousand car thefts per year: shameful, crass,
Police slow to respond, time would outpass.
Aware carjacking meant a deadly fight,
Rayhan would shield this prey with all his might.

His blood boiled hot from past theft's stinging pain,
He charged the scene to stop unlawful gain.
Leapt on one thug, kicked hard to ground the knave,
Then faced a blade that left his arm a grave.

He raised his leg, struck knife-wrist with a crack,
Sent blade ten yards through air behind his back.
A groin-kick dropped the second thief in pain,
Who had no strength to stand from where he'd lain.

Third robber charged with cleaver bright and keen,
A killer wild wolf wearing vicious mien.
Rayhan stepped back, dodged slash with subtle sway,
Prepped kick to wrist, then shots tore through the fray.

His foe fell down, by bullet struck amiss:
Fourth thug's wild shot had claimed his partner's hiss.
Next bullet struck Rayhan's left shoulder deep;
He felt warm blood in crimson currents sweep.

The gunman paused to load his weapon's round;
Three cruisers came with sirens' screaming pound.

Ambulance soon, while thugs fled past the park,
North into lanes beyond the city's dark.

At ER doors, swift paramedics rushed,
Where surgeons labored, stitching tissue hushed.
They closed the wound with needles fine and fast,
"Three weeks of calmness shall heal you at cast."

"The bullet missed your heart by grace alone;"
He lay in quiet pain's enduring moan.
Then Lilly, tearful, came to bedside stand,
Her kisses balmed him more than doctor's hand.

"My parents thank you, Father, Mother too!"
He frowned; she cried, "You saved BMW!
Not only his car, but his life—thugs slay!
That gang kills freely, every night and day."

The city's worst, police confessed outright:
Hard to arrest, let courts decide their plight.
"You faced them down; your courage broke their might;
You are my hero!" Tears shone in soft light.

Her parents lingered in the hall's dim nook,
Then slipped inside with that kind, grateful look,
Beside the bed where wounded Rayhan lay,
The mother found warm heartfelt words to say.

"Rayhan, we owe your courage, strong and deep;
You risked your life to sow and ours to reap.
God blessed our Lilly, gaining you so true;
Whate'er you choose, we'll help you see it through!

"Your futures hold our blessing, full and free,"
She vowed, absolving every past decree.
Rayhan smiled, holding his love close and tight;
Lilly wept sweet tears, bathed in golden sight.

Miracle Reunion

With daughter, son-in-law, she kept her post,
Her wheelchair fixed where healthcare mattered most.
The hospital's harsh lights burned stiff and pale,
No kindness in the air, just sterile stale.

She could not move, she could not find her place,
Just rows of anxious silent souls to face.
Her daughter signed her in with practiced grace,
Then wheeled her to some quiet, dimmer space.

Near that marked door where answers might be found,
Her eyes locked on a name that shook the ground:
"Yeffrey Dunn" stared at her in letters bold:
A shade from youth, now medical and cold.

"Not him," she whispered through a tightened throat,
"Just callous chance that wears his name-like note."
She shook her head but couldn't shake the view;
That name still cut as deep as love once knew.

The name, Yeffrey Dunn, struck like whispered fate,
A dream called out when days and nights grew late.

For forty years it hid within her heart,
A buried thorn she couldn't tear apart.

Her tears had soaked her pillow countless times,
Her guilt outlived the reach of passing rhymes.
No strength could shake this sorrow from her soul,
Its roots dug deep, beyond her self-control.

Now lost in painful thoughts of those "mad" years,
When fear and change baptized them all in sears.
Her parents, scholars, exiled from their home,
Sent north where bitter winds and sand would roam.

She with five schoolmates went at age eighteen,
To a far vill where life was hard and lean.
Her brother went where freezing winters blow,
To guard their parents through the northern snow.

Young Rosen, raised with books, not toil or strain,
Now faced a world of labor, sweat, and pain.
She cooked cornmeal and sorghum buns just plain,
But gagged and starved, her loved weight lost, health slain.

She had to haul manure in heavy pails,
Shoulders aflame, her strength too weak for sails.
She dug and spread soil mixed with horse's waste,
Hands blistered raw from hard tasks done in haste.

Then Darren Dunn, a villager, stepped near;
At twenty strong, his kindness crystal-dear.
He took her load, just asked she clean his cart;
He swung his heavy tools like martial art.

She watched his pickaxe in its graceful flight,
Loosening earth with easy, practiced might.
His shoulders bare despite the winter's chill;
His muscles taut, her heart began to fill.

How strong! How skilled! Her admiration grew;
Then no day's work would ever part the two.
He did her heavy tasks without complaint,
And turned her midnight into morning's paint.

Soon village rhythms felt like home again;
Farm tools appeared as good as the old pen.
With Dunn's strong hands to guide and ease her way,
She found her feet, and dared to hope, to stay.

As top among the schooled, she won the race
To teach the village children light and place,
Yet still with Darren shared a bond so true;
Warm laughs and good food always cheered the view.

Then came the night he knocked with troubled eyes;
"The headman's girl now wants me," came his sighs.
"Should I refuse?" Their glances locked, held tight;
Her heart screamed *no*, she wouldn't lose this light.

Could she stay here, where hardship ruled each day?
Now city's comfort just felt worlds away.
As hope for home seemed faint, one daring choice:
She leapt into his arms, let love rejoice.

They clung like vines in storms, both fierce, both young;
Their passion raw, their first sweet union sprung.
A bride by spring, by moonlit vows she swore;
Then two years more, a son they would adore.

Yeffrey Dunn came, her joy now multiplied,
With husband's love and child held to her side.
No wealth, no fame, each day her heart was full;
A new life raced between sweet home and school.

Then winds of change blew through the nation's hand;
All city youth could now return, unplanned.
Her kin were all back home, and city's door
Stood open wide if she could pass once more.

Her parents wrote, though knowing she'd been wed:
"Take the exam, or stay in want," they read.
But how? Her roots were cut by rural life;
No time to study, only stress and strife.

Her husband found the letter tucked with care,
Saw restless nights, the burden she must wear.
"I won't chain you to toil just for the grain,"
He whispered low, though love cried out in pain.

"Choose freely: if you leave, we'll sign the page;
A divorce, then, shall bring back your old stage."
She wept till dawn, her future torn in two;
The heart's fierce war no logic could construe.

Three days, then papers signed with shaking hand;
She fled at dawn through mist and fading land.
One last kiss pressed upon her sleeping boy,
Her tears the only proof of stolen joy.

"What mother leaves?" she cursed herself, undone,
As trains bore her toward the rising sun.
Her parents' home became her brittle shield,
Where books and grief fought till her fate was healed.

She passed the test, as all knew that she would;
At univ learned and walked where scholars stood.
A classmate wed, yet though their bed was shared,
No strength, no fire, just hollow nights compared.

Two daughters came, their lives her fleeting light;
She stayed till both had grown and left her sight.
At fifty-two, she cut the bloodless tie,
And let old ghosts from northern fields reply.

Now free, she dreamed of roads that led back north,
To beg their pardon, bridge the love gone forth.
But shame like ice had frozen every start:
"I'll see you where no worlds can keep apart."

The doctor's mask hid half his face from view,
Yet kindness shone in all he said and knew.
His gentle tone, his patience firm but sweet,
Made leaving harder on her feeble beat.

She thanked him, turned to leave through steady glare,
But then the name, Yeffrey Dunn, froze her stare.
"Can't be my son," she whispered, "Books were rare;
No college doors for field-worn hands to share."

But shame's old rusty chains began to break:
"What higher stake could courage undertake?"
A current surged, she turned her chair around,
Met shocked eyes over that mask tightly bound.

"Forgive me, Doctor, may we talk?" she tried;
Her voice a reed-thin whisper, trembling sighed.
He paused, looked up and answered with rare grace,
"Of course. What questions linger in your case?"

"I'm a school teacher here," she said, voice low,
"But had kin in Simsai's fields long ago.
There I wed Darren Dunn, bore one sweet son;
Then policy changed, all we were, undone!"

"Forty years lost, yet still his face I see,
And when I read your name, dear, could it be—?"
The room froze still. Her daughter gasped, confused,
While doctors' tools on trays lay dull, unused.

He sat in silence, thirty seconds passed;
Each tick a knife, she gripped her wheels, aghast.
Then came the tears behind the mask's blue veil;
His hands rose slow, revealed a face gone pale.

"I am your Yeffrey Dunn!" His chair flew wide;
"Tingawan-born! And Darren Dunn's my guide!
Why forty years? Why left your son to pine?"
Tears poured: her dam of guilt undone in shine.

The world spun black, she slumped, her daughter's grasp,
The only rope to keep her from collapse.
No mask now hid the truth: both love and blame
Had waited forty years to speak her name.

She wept, recovered, with two storms inside,
Both joy's bright surge and guilt's relentless stride.
"Not that I didn't long to hold you tight,
But shame kept me from facing love's lost light."

"Oh child, I drowned in nights of silent cries;
Failed you, your father, couldn't meet your eyes.
To see you now, so risen, so renowned,
More grace than this frail heart had ever crowned."

Then through his tears, he stepped to where she sat,
And folded her in arms with a kind pat.
She melted there, four decades torn in two,
Now stitched by sobs that shook the whole room through.

The others wept to witness love's strange math:
How forty winters burned to one warm path.
No mask, no past, no distance left to bear,
Just mother, son, and all that breath could share.

When morning rounds had ended, quiet fell;
They sought a restaurant where time could swell.
Four souls, one table, stories left to trace,
Like scattered pearls now lifted into grace.

"Aft you departed," Yeffrey spoke again,
"Dad found me that stepmom when I was ten.
She struck me all the time, then bore a girl.
The marriage cracked; love couldn't mend the curl.

"Yet Father toiled, each copper coin he'd saved,
To buy me books that built the path I craved.
"Could you—I be pardoned?" She sounded bold;
"Mom, Dad's here too," he wept, "love won't get cold!

"At seventy-two, what's time for disdain?
You claimed me fearless through your joy and pain.
That you remembered, this alone, this true,
Makes me the richest son earth ever knew."

Some days had passed before she sought her son,
And met his wife and boy, both next to none.
At last she saw Darren, her heart's own cry,
The man she'd loved through each long lonesome sky.

Their trembling arms entwined like willow strands;
He whispered peace with old familiar hands:
"No debt remains, no shadow stains our past;
The winds that tore our roots aside have passed."

Now Heaven grants this amber afternoon
To mend what storms had shattered far too soon.
Let's gather joy like spring buds after snow,
For grace arrives when we dare trust its glow.

The registry bore witness to their name,
While Rosen vowed with quiet steady flame:
"This second chance I'll weave with golden thread
To warm the hearts which pining sorrows fed."

Defiant Doctor

She sobbed for care for deadly plague affright;
Her gasping voice cut through like freezing night.
She wept for being SARS-claimed and left alone:
"They'd leave my corpse to rot on dirt or stone!"

He swore to her his clinic opened wide,
"But doctors flee, I may bring death," she cried.
"Please just relax and smile; should death come near,
The white coat means I shall die first in here."

No pause, no mask, unbent will gleamed so bright;
She cried her thanks, no more lone death to fright.
Sarah Sweety, content with joy so grand,
On Monday laughed, yet by Tuesday, near banned.

Adored as "Sars," her name now turned to gall,
For SARS the plague stole health, home, work, and all.
That February, Hong Kong's flight of dread
Brought coughs to Scarborough's hospital bed.

The new provincial law: "Chain health to bind,
Lest mercy spread the deadly plague we grind."

Tuesday's quick call: last test showed SARS's blight;
By law, she should be quarantined off sight.

She coughed, she gasped, prepared, yet knees went weak;
To be locked up meant death with no road peek.
All plague-marked souls were shunned like wartime foes,
Left starved or frozen 'neath God's blindfold throws.

She phoned her doctor asking for quick aid;
A voice replied, "By law you'll die with shade."
The hospital scoffed, "Our wards overflow;
You'd breathe your last where no one needs to know."

Four doctors fled, the fifth just heard the tone;
Now set to die alone, she dropped her phone.
She called her boyfriend, sought his heart and care;
But he became depressed and lost life stare.

Distressed Sars asked to be called *Sarah* then,
Yet steel doors slammed against her sweating pen.
To him alone could Sarah voice her pain,
"They've robbed my lungs of breath, my veins of strain."

She begged his door, his arms, but he'd turned stone:
"My lock's been changed: no key for you to bone."
"Drive me to Mom's home then," voice raw and bent;
"I'll board for New York," said he, "cash all spent."

She stood, cement-limbed, screaming in the air,
"Why now this flight? Why locks? Why vanished care?"
Last light was parents, unseen since the snows,
Their Roy Road home was where love's vine once rose.

It was a half-hour's walk for healthy pace,
But she dragged plague-hours to reach porch's place.
She knocked and sobbed she was so gravely ill;
The door soon cracked, "Sars, why court death's dark still?"

Then coughs tore loose, the cruel wood slammed hard:
"To hospital!" The blast left poor Sars scarred.
Her sobs scraped stones where parents' ghosts now stay,
A daughter's hands pressed to a glass-walled gray.

"Wait!" called her mother, voice through wood strained tight,
"There's one who fights where Western meds take flight.
Wise Doctor Liu, his needles pierce the grim.
His phone: nine-two-nine-nine, the rest's with him."

"But can such pricks tame viruses?" she cried.
"Now fly! His name's online!" the door replied.
"And Mom, no more *Sars*!" "Then go, child, just go!"
The porch wept silence, while roads moaned below.

Hope's ember dimmed, she dialed work's cold gate;
"The Act forbids return until you're straight."

Outside, Toronto's breath turned iron-black;
No bed, no bread, no cure to fight attack.

Suicide whispered; then, only needle's chance;
Some unknown Liu, she clawed at fate's last lance.
Two codes: four-one-six's well-known domain;
Or six-four-seven, new like spring's first rain.

She pieced the digits with smart number art:
Three tries, and *click*; then back to poem's start.

At one, she burned on Liu's thin bed, so pale;
His needles stirred her up for that swift hail.
Through subtle skill, they wove her breath anew,
Till sleep, long lost, returned on golden dew.

An hour passed, then she woke: her veins sang light,
As herbs steeped dawn in cups of bitter might.
Three days: cough ceased, throat cooled, high fever gone;
Nine more, till Liu proclaimed her free from dawn.

Nightmare dissolved to sunlit, waking bliss,
His needles leading time back into kiss.
Yet Sarah ne'er knew Liu had caught her blight;
That first lung-reek stung hard his nose's height.

No mask—he'd none, just silver needles' gleam,
In half an hour, his breath turned stagnant stream.
Stuffed nose, choked air, sharp SARS's claws took hold;
He flicked in own flesh needles well controlled.

He drank the potion, herbs boiled black and deep;
A fever burned a day, then fell to sleep.
For twelve long days, his healing arts he plied,
Until the day she rose, and Liu's foe died.

"You are a *real* doctor!" Her tears were caught;
He smiled, unskilled at titles honor-wrought.
"Sir, you scorn grave!" He swore, "You're mine to keep;
If death knocks once, I'll greet it at your deep."

His gaze held hers, a kindness soft yet clear.
She fell into his arms, too stunned to tear.
Long silence, then, "My life is yours," she pled.
"Be mine." He froze; her heart beat wild, fear fled.

What sweetness, saving one near death's grim gate!
What shock, to hear love's plea mid healing's fate!
"My dear, I can't, though joy crowns your new life."
She cried bright grief: at him, at her, at strife.

"My path says no, though angels marked you *starred*,"
She raged at suns that left her world ice-scarred.

Hero's Heart

He knew SARS killed, a plague both grave and dire;
He saw the gasping patient, felt death's fire.
No doctors dared to take her fading breath,
Yet he said, "Come," and braced for his own death.

No mask, no shield, just needles, herbs, and art;
His hands fought fate while time stood stark and heart.
The woman lived, his miracle complete,
Yet that still scared friends stunned by SARS' defeat.

"Why took such risk for one all others fled?
No gear, no hope—'twas death you might have wed."
He answered firm, "A healer's vow takes flight;
We meet the grave to spare our charge its night.

"Not textbook words, but bone-deep creed I keep;
Recall Japan, that broadcaster in the deep.
She warned the town 'Run! Run!' as best she plead;
Her voice drowned fast, yet lives rose where she freed.

"So, too, my call: Contagion breeds no dread;
I treat all souls the same when death draws head."

His friends, now hushed, all glimpsed with sudden start
A patient's banner praising his kind heart:

"A model doctor, flawless in his care;
No other matches how his needles dare."

A Shining Father[1]

Huang Qiao stood frozen, hearing the hall's roar;
"Now freeze," she cried, "or you will taste your sore!"
His third wife chased their son with whip held high;
The boy fled fast while father wondered why.

He hid behind his dad in sudden fright:
"I tried to catch the cock that jumped in flight.
Why mind my business, my mother dear?"
"Damn little bastard!" flew her frozen tear.

"You damned old crone!" the angry boy shot back;
"How dare you!" father seized him mid-attack.
"Such vile contempt! What will become of you?"
The boy broke free with fury's raging view.

---

[1] This poem is based on a true account drawn from several sources made available in Chinese on the internet by Huang Zhangfa and Huang Yonghui, among others. Descendants of the Huang family can use this poem for noncommercial purposes as long as due credit is given to the author, Harry J. Huang (黃俊雄).

He started roaring, rolling on the floor,
Made utmost scene to settle vengeance score.
A smart spoiled child did not know right from sin,
Yet parents must endure his wretched din.

The father stomped, his face with blood aflame,
"Kneel now before your mother! Bear your shame!"
To kneel, a punishment both harsh and deep,
In those days e'en made hardened elders weep.

"I played with rooster, what is wrong for real?"
The boy defied, "No way, I just won't kneel!"
"Dare you resist?" the father roared, fist high,
To strike the child beneath the household sky.

The mother, fearful, pled with frantic voice,
"My fault: poor training spared this brush with choice!
Let me withdraw and discipline him right;"
But father countered, "No, he'll feel my might!"

"Then do your worst," she yielded, cold, resigned,
As father thundered, "Kneel!" with will unkind.
The boy relented, "Since you force my knee—"
When cane tapped floor, grandsire was there to see.

"Oh, why this storm?" he asked. "What can he learn,
So young, to earn such severe shocking burn?"

The boy flew fast behind his grandsire's side,
That favored child who knew his cherished pride.

"See now?" he dared. "I'll never bow and kneel!
If you hit me, my grandsire'll make you feel!"
The father raged, ashamed before the crowd:
His small son dared defy him, proud and loud.

Punish the child? Grandfather's pride aggrieved;
Ignore the act? Worse mischief soon conceived.
Huang Qiao endured the painful piercing way,
Found blame in parents, not the child's wild play.

Three wives bore many children, wild, untrained,
No discipline imposed, no order gained.
Now clarity struck hard: they craved decree:
Strong family rules that'd restrict their free.

Grandfather took the boy and left the hall;
Then Huang Qiao asked his wife to narrate all.
"What happened here when I arrived today?"
She told the tale in sorrowful display.

"He found cockfighting crowds on threshing ground,
Near paddy fields, where raucous shouts resound.
He chased a rooster, sought to join the fray,
But swift it fled, refusing capture's sway.

"At slightest touch, the bird took wing in fright,
Flapped past the hall into bedchamber's night.
It leapt on dresser, flew to bed's embrace,
And wreaked pure havoc in that sacred space.

"It soiled quilts, net, knocked candles to the floor,
And smashed blue floral vase, pain over sore.
I chased him, blamed him for the bird's offense;
He fled like prey through terror's fevered sense.

"In hall I caught him after strain and fight,
But ere I struck, he slipped into the light.
Just then you entered, witnessed his escape;
Big chaos caused by panicked rooster's scrape."

The whole event renewed an old alarm,
When first wife visited her parents' farm.
Her eldest son, who traveled by her side,
Met cousin, fell in love at just first tide.

He led her to the orchard and picked pears,
Began their courtship while enjoying their shares
The mother warned with strict command severe:
"No cousin dating!" banned with chilling fear.

He scorned her words, declared his heart's domain,
Rejected meddling in his private gain.

She cut the visit short, brought him back home;
Such bold disobedience should never roam.

The more Huang Qiao thought on these twined alarms,
The more his soul feared deep for future harms.
He called his three wives, seeking order's plan:
Rules for sons, later twenty-one in clan.

In Huang Qiao's school where youthful minds were bred,
Firm codes were forged for paths that lay ahead.
The young must have behavior rules for life;
Each should achieve clear goals despite all strife.

At once he penned guidelines designed to reign,
Soon seventeen rules set in ordered train.
Each "Father says" left no room for debate;
The headers of three words would then dictate.

"Memorize all!" the stern command rang clear,
His sons were all advised to hold them dear.
Recitation thus dawned with dread spread wide;
No son could chant the lengthy rules' full tide.

The first son spoke eight laws, his voice held fast;
Next one took Ninth rule, but Fourteenth his last.
Third tried Fifteen to Seventeen's domain,
But somehow stumbled through with wrenching pain.

The father frowned at answers, flawed and fleet,
But stayed his hand and spared the threatened beat.
The strict rules broke 'neath memory's firm hold;
And some stretched on for thirty lines when told.

The stiff and slow recitation prevailed;
The rules appeared to work and never failed.
No son misbehaved e'er since guides began;
This comfort greatly warmed the anxious man.

He chose to revise rules for ease of mind,
To lodge in memory, clear and designed.
For one long year he pondered, watched, refined,
Based on his sons' respect for rules behind.

At last, twenty-one guides in rhyme he cast,
With opening verse and a final blast.
He read them loud till tone and tune sufficed,
Then announced Huang's Guidelines,[2] no pain disguised:

1
First, cherish well the nature of our bond;
Read "Lu E,"[3] the fine poem that'd respond.

---

[2] The restriction of the source text has resulted in many imperfect iambic feet in the translation of the following twenty-one poems where the typical iamb is altered.
[3] This poem expresses children's gratitude to parents for their upbringing.

Dad toiled with strength, his life as hard as stone;
Mom nursed you till her energy was blown.
Yu's Shun[4] tilled land, yet was praised as the best;
Zhong You's[5] care for his mom surpassed the rest.
E'en young lambs to their mothers kneel[6] in grace;
Above all, strive to be a good son's place.

2

Next, always hold the ethics of mankind;
Be joyful, striving brothers of the kind.
Observe the ranks—eldest first and youngest last,
Create a bond where respect is steadfast.
Rich brothers shan't despise a needy one;
Remember your bond if one needs a bun.
The dodder and pine grow into one tree;
Greet siblings on the road and do not flee.

---

[4] Emperor Shun of Yu State was extremely poor during his childhood, but he was such a good son that his filiality impressed Heaven, and then a celestial elephant and a celestial bird came to help him with his farming.

[5] If space permitted, the original line might be rendered as follows: Zhong You (also known as Zi Lu, one of Confucius' disciples), who ate coarse food but often carried rice home for his mother from more than 50 kilometers away, is a role model for you and your brothers.

[6] Translator's notes: (1) That young lambs kneel when being fed by their mother is interpreted in the Chinese culture as a gesture of gratitude. (2) The translator regrets that the limited space of this line does not accommodate the words of the second half of the source line that says wild ducks also feed back their old mothers, and that a mere summary translation approach has been taken, resulting in the loss of some details. This may also be found elsewhere in the English translation of the behavior guidelines.

3
Third, keep your self-image in the best light;
Be lively, neat and cheerful day and night.
Sit straight and stand with grace, respect wise friends;
Refinement helps you make amends, not bends.
Snakes coil and stretch, then straighten in their time;
Small insects change from slush to form in rhyme.
When you become a father on some date,
Serve gladly as a bowl, a pot, a plate.

4
Fourth, remember that in your years of prime
You must not be a weak man anytime.
Show both your strength and softness as you need;
Then you will be a man that all will heed.
Embrace the wisdom of the past with zest;
Pursue the ancient sages who are best.
Outdated ways and low moods are your foe;
Keep striving hard to put on your best show.

5
Fifth, you must manage well the cash you spend;
There'll be many events you need attend.
Be frugal and watch closely what you buy;
An overjoyed guest has the last reply.
We toil each day for food and clothes we wear;
A lazy man will find no place to share.

Don't waste your funds on things you do not need;
If you are poor, then seeking help is freed.

6
Sixth, do not be a pedant anywhere;
For any pedant finds no thoroughfare.
Study hard with high ambitions in mind;
Leave ignorance and folly both behind.
A life of ease is hard to keep in sight;
But precious knowledge gained will bring you light.
Though poor, Li Mi and Mai Chen[7] reached great goal:
They read books from ox horn and shoulder pole.

7
Seventh, keep all bad habits far away;
Work hard, avoid waste; happy you will stay.
Drink in small sips if you have wine in store;
Don't shop on credit when funds are no more.
Gambling is never the right path to choose;
Sleeping in will cause your marriage to lose.
Time flies just like a shooting star in sky;
Don't be a flower that blooms just to die.

---

[7] If space were not limited, this couplet could be translated as follows: If Li Mi of the Sui Dynasty (581 – 618) and Zhu Mai Chen of the Western Han Dynasty (206 BC – AD 24), who were born into poor farmers' families, had simply accepted their fate instead of studying hard, they would never have reached their status of nobility! Li Mi was seen reading books hanging on an ox's horn while he was herding cattle. Zhu Mai Chen was reading his books hanging on the shoulder pole while he was carrying large loads of wood.

8
Eighth, take charge of your home and have your say,
Beware of the roles man and woman play.
Prevent quarrels like those from neighbor B;
Do the same kind deeds done by neighbor C.
Heaven showers on *liyi*[8] homes joy and health;
A harmonious home brings bliss and wealth.
A soft voice frees your home of woes oft known;
A good son'll have fine children of his own.

9
Ninth's about family chores in a chain:
Home's easy to start, yet hard to sustain.
Watch every lamp and candle that gives light;
Secure each gate and lock the door at night.
Fix roof leaks promptly when they come in sight;
All fallen fences should be mended right.
Assign each child their tasks when skies are bright;
Gather your cows and sheep, sleep free of fright.

10
Tenth, read Ten Poems together, line by line;
Some may seem unpolished, yet they all shine.
Enjoy the subtle beauty that they yield;
Learn hidden meanings from each verse revealed.

---

[8] *Liyi* (禮儀) in *pinyin*, which means etiquette and rituals, is used to accommodate the number of syllables of the line.

Care for your mother when she's growing old;
Officials should have bigger hearts of gold.
This yet does not express all I would say;
May you come to understand me one day!

11
Elev'nth, don't be an overbearing man,
But serve the people kindly as you can.
Condemned officials find no place to hide;
A great name lives forever, far and wide.
Do not abuse your best and noble days;
Hot-headedness will only lead to strays.
Earth has seen many heroes live and die;
What you loathe is gossip fly'ng in the sky.

12
Twelfth, I would love to see the Huang clan grow;
My brothers, sons, and grandsons make us glow.
Branch rivers flow forth from the same clear source;
Trees spread from the same roots by nature's force.
Don't offend Emperors where'er you are;
Be humble to others, both near and far.
A home with peace and harmony will thrive;
Pass on forebears' morals, keep them alive

13
Thirteenth, always be an honest, good man;
Be fair with everyone, make each a fan.
Help relatives and friends who are in need;

Don't shun a neighbor who has eaten seed.
Harmony's a wonderful thing in life;
Endurance and patience are pride's midwife.
Teachings from ancestors are worth their gold;
Take right path, and you'll face no woe or scold.

14
Fourteenth, when you do business outside,
Don't mistreat partners; don't fight and don't chide.
Share profits fairly in your hawking trade;
Don't cheat the old and the young who need aid.
Birds rest in trees before the last sun ray;
Rise at cockcrow to begin each new day.
Read classic lines of poetry all your life;
They guard you from risks better than a knife.

15
Fifteenth, don't indulge in a life of ease;
Tolerate others for the sake of peace.
Entertain guests with wine that you have stored;
Shun officials if you have no gold hoard.
Humble yourself to neighbors—no hauteur;
Accept kin and friends, be they rich or poor.
Embrace what Heaven has arranged for you;
The Three Precepts can be followed as due.

16
Sixteenth, don't fight for whatever appeals;
Endurance and honesty are great deals.

Land passed to young generation holds weight,
But etiquette also makes a fine estate.
Most important, always obey the law;
Make me proud and never commit a flaw.
I ponder on my past and find my life
A lawful, diligent one without strife.

17
Seventeenth, know that in life wisdom leads;
Precaution and caution prevent misdeeds.
A man's heart is like a dagger in dark;
Crises arise, like chess games you would mark.
Great ambition seeks advice from wise friends;
Guard against bandits and devilish ends.
You may be all right if you have some cash;
If you've spent it all, quickly they will dash.

18
Eighteenth, always watch what you do and say;
In this cold world, we play the minion's way.
With good friends, you enjoy toast after toast;
In unwanted talk, one word matters most.
If blessed, you will find life a joyful feast;
If unblessed, you'll find it worse than a beast.
Trouble often starts from unneeded talk;
Once mishaps befall you, you'll be in shock.

19
Nineteenth, nurture fine traits as best you can;
Always strive to be an outstanding man.
In cold winter, wear warm fur and no tat;
In hot summer, sleep on a bamboo mat.
Preserve filial piety you can vaunt;
Smart children and grandkids are what you want.
Be a Confucian, steadfast and renowned;
We, father and son, are forever bound.

20
Twentieth, here's advice that may make you bored:
Don't do a thing that you cannot applaud.
Careful second thoughts keep you safe and sound,
But you gain from pain when mistakes are found.
Live a leisurely life, resentment freed;
Loyalty's foe is ignorance and greed.
Nothing from harming others will you gain;
Honest men survive tough times without pain.

21
Twenty-first, out my last advice will stand;
I hope none of my sons will ruin my land.
Prioritize the needed cash and grain;
Pay all your taxes early, free of pain.
Children owe parents a mountain of thanks;
Husband and wife's love fills oceans and banks.

I cannot set in script all I would say;
Therefore to thee these thoughts I do relay.

Huang Qiao thought rhyming rules would stick in mind;
With practice done, he called the sons assigned.
To hall they came, revised rules there to say;
And as expected, well performed that day.

But as they stood, two sons had nervous air,
While rooster-chaser showed no thought or care.
This lack of heed offended father's view;
"Recite now, you!" his stern command broke through.

To his surprise, that bright-eyed boy spoke clear;
'Twas fluent, graceful, pride and joy shone dear.
His brothers tried, both spoke the same whole guide;
Though less with grace, their verses still stretched wide.

The father marveled at the young boy's skill,
Yet comfort found the others climbed the hill.
Indeed he loved the young one's keen display,
But peace still bloomed where elders won the day.

What their rules expected the sons all knew
And just behaved as they were taught to do.
The father aged while sons grew tall and strong;
"What splendid household!" neighbors praised along.

They studied hard, revered each guiding sage,
Loved young and old, showed kindness at life's stage.
The model youths became a brilliant brand;
Huang's kin rose rich, renowned 'cross every land.

Life peaceful for the Huang's esteemed demesne,
Till father's eightieth year brought strain and pain.
In finest silks, all kin assembled bright,
For joyous feast in holiday's delight.

They knew his wisdom, felt his love's embrace;
But then confusion struck each anxious face.
Midst celebration's mirth and banquet cheer,
Huang called for silence, piercing every ear.

"See courtyard swallows, live with ease bestowed?
Yet mountain kin survive harsh wild's hard road!"
He paused, then warned of softened wings untried:
"Comfort breeds weakness, challenges denied.

"For greatness, seek your own self-reliant way;"
He then stunned all, "Go build new homes today!
Leave now, sons twenty-one! Depart this stead,
Find foreign soil to plant your future's bed."

The eldest son opposed, "Sire, old and gray,
If all sons vanish, who will show your sway?

What use are sons so vast in numbered claim,
Who can't attend your frame and guard your fame?"

Huang's words shocked all, the gathering stunned still,
While three wives voiced their heartfelt dread and chill.
"But you grow old and lost strength can't regain;"
They urged, "You need care, let some sons remain!"

He gazed at sons, emotion deep and tried:
"I'd keep you near till death beside me bide.
But times are fraught, here dwelling risks increase;
To seek new homes brings safety, peace, release.

"I served the Emperor long in war's dismay,
And marched through frontiers where wild lands hold sway.
Take wives and children, settle where you choose;
Rich, untamed earth awaits the plow's deep use."

Huang scanned his wives, their age in silver traced;
"Each keep your eldest son," his voice firm-paced.
"To tend your mother's twilight days with grace;
The rest seek homes beyond this strife-torn place."

He split his wealth: eighty thousand *guan*[9] bright,
With gold, silver, eight hundred *chen*[10] in sight.

---

[9] A unit of 1000 copper coins.
[10] A unit of approximately 400 grams.

The twenty-one sons, each received a share;
His hopes were open, treatment kind and fair.

To eighteen leaving, steeds of strength he gave,
To bear them toward new lands they would crave.
To every son, a fam'ly tree was told,
To guard their roots in each new foreign hold.

All hearts hung heavy, tears on cheeks did flow;
Wives, daughters wept, yet trust lay firm below.
For this must be the best path to embrace;
Or father's wisdom would not set this pace.

He tended every need, each son's desire:
Their wealth, their frame, their souls by love's kind fire.
His last words chimed in poem's hallowed rhyme,
"Farewell to Sons"[11] for all their future time.

---

[11] This translation by Harry J. Huang is based on the Chinese version from Jieyang, China. It was first published in *The Beautiful and the Absurd: Stories for Our Times*, but has been edited. As mentioned in that book, the original Chinese by Huang Qiao was an oral farewell that was believed to have been transcribed by the twenty-one sons afterward and then passed onto their own children and grandchildren, generation after generation, which appears to have resulted in the different versions that exist today. The original poem was untitled. All Chinese titles and translated titles were added later mostly by his descendants. The title "Farewell to Departing Sons" briefly appeared in the sample copies of the fiction work, but "Farewell to Sons" is what this author uses, though it may differ from some lengthy Chinese titles.

Your strong horses will take you to new land;
Settle in any fine place you'd demand.
Stay in the new land as if it's your own;
It will be just like the old home you've known.
Remember my farewell words day and night;
Burn incense for ancestors each twilight.
May Heaven bless my sons, twenty and one;
You shall all thrive and shine like the bright sun.

This poem served as code for kin to trace,
The Huang clan's ID key through time and space.
Eighteen sons now fanned out to seek new ground,
Each calmly claimed his land where hope was found.

Two years returned, reunion's warm embrace;
Huang Qiao rejoiced at every brave son's grace.
As he foresaw, they thrived, not just survived;
In new hamlets, prosperity derived.

Farewell to Sons

Original Chinese by HUANG Qiao (黃峭, 872 – 953) [Jieyang Version]
English Translation by Harry J. HUANG (黃俊雄 1956 –)

Not long after, Huang Qiao found peaceful rest;
In sleep, no pain, God kindly took him blessed.
As coffin moved to destined graveyard's stead,
Abruptly sun went black, dark thunders bred.

Rain poured in floods, and lightning tore the sky;
The pallbearers left coffin high and dry.
On slope they sheltered till the storm ceased blow;
The sun returned above bright beaming glow.

They rushed back, but lost coffin in their care;
"Good Heaven! Where is it?" they cried out scare.
"Could thieves have stolen?" None would dare such fate;
A coffin's curse just boded death to mate!

Through frantic search, shocked eyes could scarce believe:
A mountain crack, deep as a cavern's sleeve!
It swallowed coffin whole, in earth's deep maw,
Though grave-site breached the custom and raw law.

Sons begged pallbearers to reclaim the dead,
But Taoist halted them with wisdom bred:
"No! Heaven's will! Let sky-burial stand!"
They filled the rift with each obedient hand.

Then sealed crack, ancient grave with soil piled high,
Moved stones, raised tomb beneath the watching sky.

All done by Taoist craft, precise and grand,
A wonder worthy of this royal land.

News spread like wind through far and near domains,
"Was Huang Qiao Heaven's man?" asked field and lanes.
No answer came, yet Huang's bright sons arose:
Most served the emperor who sealed their prose.

The rest held posts of state with steadfast worth;
Each title but meant grandeur in their birth.
They were renowned officials hailed great men,
Whom common folk would praise time and again.

Time surely flies! If curious, you'd be told
Of Huang's vast kin; ten hundred years unfold.
One thousand seventy since his grace day,
His poem lives where seventeen million pray.

From homeland's shore to every foreign place,
They bear the line of Huang's enduring grace.
They chant the verse that ancient voices taught,
And live the laws that order every thought.

The poem's bloom, a hundred versions gained,
Each subtle change a living branch sustained.
When read aloud, descendants know their root,
In phrase or pause, an ancestor's pursuit..

Each year, from every walk, they journey far
To Shaowu's mountain, peaceful e'ergreen star.
Before Huang Qiao's grand tomb, they bend in grace,
Connecting lives to forefather's embrace.

He dreamed great kin: now millions stand renewed;
A smiling earth now wears a grateful mood.
What miracle man! What miracle line!
A family all forged by love divine!

Radiant Ray

Green paddy fields from Ferry Dock stretched wide,
To meet the sky in blue and verdant stride.
Hot summer breezes rustled seedlings dance
And stirred green waves that cooled in each advance.

Harsh thirty-nine degrees made farmers stare;
Thick plants and water chilled the scorching air.
A frog croaked once, then countless voices swelled;
They chorused far and near, through fields they dwelled.

The southern winds rippled the green expanse,
Divided by streams under willows' glance.
On trees cicadas chirped clear rhythmic sound,
A contrast in the quiet as noon found.

Two hundred spaces south from river's side,
There Plum Village with crimson blossoms vied.
In the vill dwelled Huang Shaohui (黃紹輝), Shining Ray,
Herbalist who could blast all ills away.

A one-man hospital for womb and bone,
He healed heads and hearts, and broke fears' throne.

He cured what others fled, no ill too vast,
Called "Half-Celestial" by the thanks amassed.

To strangers: "Doctor Huang," or "Doctor Ray,"
But Plum folk hailed him in a warmer way.
His peers cried "Brother Ray!" with warm embrace;
The young called "Uncle Ray!" with childlike grace.

Yet "Farmer" he proclaimed, both plain and true,
As rare as cures he would with pride pursue.
In humble boots, not in doctor's attire,
He lit hope's flame from earth and herbal fire.

No formal school of med'cine marked his days;
No degree conferred in old-fashioned ways.
His learning's source remained a secrete sealed,
He read the classics, wisdom stood revealed.

He penned the Herbal Rhymes, that guide so bright,
Every herb's nature capped in verse's light.
No professor e'er matched this tome's design:
For trainee herbalists, a divine sign.

His clinic was a home of purpose, unfeigned,
Where herbs were ground, ills treated, students trained.
No fixed fee charged, just nickels, dimes conveyed,
Or live chicken, fish freshly caught, not weighed.

The poor paid naught, no grievance stirred his soul;
His joy in cures made broken bodies whole.
"When patients smile, the doctor smiles" he swore;
This truth he lived, now timeless evermore.

One early spring, a couple, tense and worn,
Arrived with crying babe, forlorn, forsworn.
"Uncle Ray," the mom wept, "no stool for days,
My baby's face now bumped in painful blaze."

Ray checked the skin, the eyes, the mouth with care,
Then told them, "Need earthworms now, not despair.
Bring seven to nine, with thy babe returned."
"Earthworms?" The father frowned, concern unearned.

He rushed back home, dug dirt with hoe's sharp sweep,
Caught seven slender creeps from earth heaps deep.
When they returned, Ray set three worms below
Upon the navel, capped with warming glow.

"All done," said Ray. "No drug or potion craved."
"But Uncle Ray—" "He'll poop tonight," he braved.
They left, reluctant, doubt their hearts still knit,
Yet they just had to trust cures Ray saw fit.

"Will this cure work?" the wife demanded, fraught,
As homeward path their anxious steps had brought.

The husband said, "Ray holds remedies rare,
For strange diseases, just beyond compare.

"He's practiced medicine through age-long trust;
Half-God, remember, dear! Doubt not, we must!"
Two days thereafter, mother beamed her way
To Ray, with such relief like dawn of May.

"My baby passed just one hour since your aid,
Now all is good and sound as I had prayed!
Thank you, dear Uncle Ray!" emotion soared;
He smiled; no words were said, yet joy outpoured.

When thanks were given, silence he preferred,
That smile conveyed what never could be heard:
Each patient knew, beneath his gentle gaze,
Their wellness lit his heart in quiet blaze.

"Uncle Ray!" cried a girl, sixteen and fair,
Just as the young mother left, unaware.
"What may I do for you?" Ray asked with care.
"I'm in distress," she wept in dark despair.

She wiped her tears upon her sleeve's rough thread,
But still they flowed like rivers, hot and red.
"Look at my eye! This pimple gives me dread!
No man will wed me if scarred here," she said.

"My lid deformed, a monster I will be!
Oh, save me, Uncle Ray, I beg of thee!"
"Relax, I'll fix it." Calm as summer's sea;
"Fix it?" she gasped, face pale, as pale may be.

"Will you cut it away?" Voice trembling, thin;
"Like my poor cousin, cursed beneath her skin.
That scar wrecked life though beauty once did win;
Once fairest rose, now pierced by grief's sharp pin."

"At thirty-five, unwed, called monster still,"
She sobbed afresh, bent to despair's dark will.
"I'd rather lose a foot! Cure this foul ill!"
Ray sought wife's sewing basket, calm and chill.

He soon returned with thread, the healing key:
"Raise this hand, show your fingers straight to me,"
She gave her hand, compliant, trusting, free.
He tied the ox-knot plain for her to see.

"Your treatment's done," he said. "Go home you may."
"What's this?" she frowned, where thread-marked finger lay.
Confused by cure so simple, plain as hay:
No blade, no balm to drive her fear away.

She felt the thread pulled tight, a binding strain,
A small discomfort, born of hope and pain.
"But will this *work*, dear Uncle Ray?" she cried,
"Won't you give medicines to stem this tide?

"At least some salve to put upon the sore,
To fight the blemish pressing at hope's door?"
"No need," said Ray, as he rose from his seat;
"Go home, relax, and trust in healing's feat."

Reluctant, she stepped out, her mind a storm:
What could this thread achieve, so plain, so warm?
She watched him fetch it from the sewing nook;
No balm it bore, no cure in thread's plain look.

Could magic hide where no herbs lay in wait?
Or will this pause but seal my cruel fate?
Ten steps away, she whirled in doubt's sharp grip,
Turned back to plead with trembling, tearful lip.

"But Uncle Ray, what if this cure should fail?
If pimple bursts, I'd be on deadly sail.
I beg you, give me medicines to arm!"
He met her fear with wisdom's steadfast calm.

"You *must* trust me. Your tears but feed the blight.
You're not the first I've guided through this night.
My cure stands perfect, faultless in its art;
This thread expels the swelling at its start.

"It stops the blemish growing fierce and deep;
Keep tight, don't touch, though comfort seems asleep.
In days, you'll wake to find the terror gone;
Your faith and thread shall greet the healing dawn."

"Oh, thank you," whispered she, though worry stayed;
Since Ray seemed sure, her doubt began to fade.
She turned to leave, but paused at his wood gate,
Almost begged drugs to soothe her fearful state.

Five eves beyond, she brought a carp's bright gleam,
Smiling the whole long way like sun through stream.
"Behold! No trace remains of fear's grim mark;
This fish thanks painless cure, your healing spark."

Yet wonder stayed: "How could mere thread untie
That swollen threat beneath my trembling eye?"
Ray smiled, "Call it thread-acupuncture's grace,
Like needles' art, but past your learning's trace.

"Rejoice! You're healed," Ray beamed with quiet cheer.
She thought, *Half-God! His title's truth shines clear.*
As footsteps turned to leave his humble door,
A new-faced grief knocked, pleading help once more.

"Please save my son, Doctor!" the mother cried,
"In hospital, hope's final ember died.
His hands grew stiff, drawn back in pain's hard bow;
He cannot lift them, death draws near him now.

"You are Half-God! You must restore his breath;
No other hand can steal him back from death!"

"Calm down," Ray said with kindness in his gaze,
"Tell how this darkness set your soul ablaze."

"Strong as an ox, but past month's waning light,
While working 'neath the trees on mountain height,
Caterpillars dropped, venom's fell from pine,
On him and one more youth, by death's design.

"First rashes burned, then torment fierce and deep;
They lost all hold where agony did creep.
In county hospital they both now lie;
My boy's hands fail—" she stopped with broken sigh.

She fell to grief, yet Ray had to see case:
Could cure be ever won in time's short race?
"I pledge no cure," he cautioned, voice low-toned,
"But take me there, let truth be known, not moaned."

"Yes! Yes! My deepest thanks!" Her voice a prayer,
She longed to kneel in worship then and there.
But moments screamed, no second left to spare;
Two bicycles soon cut the summer air.

They rode swift paths to where the sick boy stayed,
On backseats borne through twilight's paling shade.
They sped to hospital through dusk's dim glade;
Half-God and mother, hope's last pact displayed.

"I cannot treat your son," Ray told them plain,
Beside the ward where hope had turned to pain.
"He's bound by rules where Western doctors reign;
My hands are tied by hospital's cold chain."

"He worsens every hour!" the mother's cry;
"Without your aid, our boy will surely die!"
Her tears fell free as terror filled the air:
A son lost if none answered parents' prayer.

"If trust is full, and mine the only care,
Then break his bonds, no other treatments bear.
Leave this white house, its potions, and its chart;
My herbs alone must mend this poisoned part."

"Of course! Of course!" They clutched at mercy's hand,
"He'll be out now! We heed your firm command!"
Three thanks they gave, three hopes set free from night;
Half-God now held their future in his sight.

By bicycle, Ray rode through fading light;
Soon came the youth, bent, trembling, ghostly white.
His hands clenched back like claws to heaven's dome,
A sight to chill the bravest hearts that roam.

Ray checked his pulse, his tongue, his fevered state,
Knew why the learned cure had come too late.
He brewed both draughts to drink and balms to spread;
Ten days would lift this living from the dead.

But joy, once bloomed, met sorrow's bitter rain:
News came of youth in hospital's domain.
He'd died of venom no white coat could tame,
While Ray's cure spared a life from death's dark claim.

How grief tore through the parents left behind!
If only they had known where help to find!
That Half-God walked in mountains, not in books;
They wept o'er grave where pine-cursed spirit looks.

Though grief for their lost son would never fade,
Ray found a mentor's role he timely played.
He shared his precious methods, tried and true,
The herbs that healed, for every healer's view.

"The pine caterpillar's venom's real core,"
He taught, "is acid, like all insect gore.
Neutralize *that* with herbs that balance well,
Or else the wound may plunge to death's dark hell."

To doctors first, then townsfolk, he made clear
How venom's acid grip might disappear.
And after that, no deaths were seen again;
His wisdom freed the land from poison's bane.

Ray worked like some great hospital in stride,
No rest, no pause, with duty as his guide.

On New Year's Eve, as feast was laid in sight,
A neighbor's scream cut through the festive night.

"My daughter-in-law burns! Please help with might!
The pressure cooker burst, she's lost to fright!"
Ray dropped his meal: "Where lies she? Bring her here!"
"My son bears her, now! Now there! She draws near!"

A ghastly sight, the bride of one moon's grace,
Her once fair face was scorched beneath its base.
Blisters like eggs or beans swelled fierce and deep;
Forehead and eyelids burned in pain's harsh keep.

But Ray kept salves for every wound and ache;
His Rescue Cream saved her for mercy's sake.
For fire or blast, no other could compare;
This balm of life was waiting, cool and fair.

He pricked each blister with a needle's trace,
Then smoothed the cream on her discolored face.
He wrapped her face where burns stretched vast and grim;
One dose used all the cream he kept for limb.

To pharmacies he rushed, bought herbs anew,
Brewed greater batches, strong and pure and true.
No infection dared loom beneath his hand;
Her healing bloomed across the ravaged land.

Eight days had passed; she walked with parents near;
No bandage bound, and no infection's fear.
Her face, though dark as oak, which once was fair,
Showed healing's price borne deep with patient care.

The flesh had felt the brutal fire's fierce breath,
A scorching touch that flirted close with death.
Without his timely skill, infection's band
Would scar her lids and blight that youthful brand.

"Your hue returns, though slow as seasons' tide,"
Ray pledged. "With time, fair tones will bloom inside."
She thanked him, saved from ruin's bitter trace:
Her joy a balm for every wounded place.

"What payment asks your art and herbs?" she cried.
"Just thirty yuan,"[12] Ray's kindly calm replied.
A weight for neighbors, paid with grumbling sound;
They called it costly for their humble ground.

The mother-in-law spoke for all to hear;
As Ray's wife passed, she aimed the poisoned spear.
"He charged us *thirty yuan*! A sum absurd!
For treating burns, no wiser, harsher word!"

---

[12] Worth approximately US$4.00, on an exchange rate of 7.50 yuan for one US dollar.

His wife stormed home: "How dare you charge so dear?
This strains our bonds: their hardship's crystal clear!"
"I know it stings," Ray said, "yet mark this well:
The herbs alone cost more than what I tell.

"No fee I took for my hours lost to balm,
For grinding roots to bring this healing calm.
The hospital would claim two thousand more,
And leave her scarred behind its sterile door."

His wife fell silent, torn 'twixt right and grace,
Upset by neighbor's cold, accusing face.
Ray spoke no more, but turned to work undone;
New fights still waited to be fought and won.

The next day brought a worker, limping slow,
From Farm Machine Works, bearing pain's harsh blow.
His leg was burned by red-hot iron's spray;
'Twas furnace molten cast that seared his way.

Black, sticky tar now caked his ravaged skin;
'Twas used when brutal pain first did begin.
No salve was near to soothe the raging heat;
His flesh cried out in agony complete.

Coworkers first poured water, cold and sharp,
To quench the burn's deep, unforgiving spark.
But still the torment raged, a vicious flame;
Their cooling efforts failed to block its claim.

Then one man ran to buy some burn cream near,
From shops beside their factory, void of fear.
While others fanned the wound with hurried breath,
Their labor wasted, fighting fiery death.

When cream arrived, they squeezed each tube all dry,
And spread it thick where blistered flesh did lie.
But still the pain roared like a storm's wild gale;
No comfort came, no efforts could prevail.

Then tar was pressed in wild, despairing base,
To shield the burn no other cure could chase.
His flesh was charred, a truly grisly sight;
There just his strength kept conscious for the fight.

So fierce the hurt, he nearly passed out cold;
A strong man tested, courage fiercely bold.
Then one coworker spoke of Ray's great skill:
A healer who could mend and cure each ill.

He came at once, though pain tore through his stride,
To seek the cure where hope might still reside.
Though terror screamed, he limped toward the light,
To hands that healed and made the world all right.

With tender care, Ray stripped the tar's dark trace;
He soon revealed wounds that spanned leg's grim space.
He smoothed his miracle cream, cool and deep
Where burns had screamed, sweet silence bloomed in sleep.

The young man sighed as torment fled its throne,
And swift relief ran through each aching bone.
The gauze wrapped round the tortured limb so thin;
Pants clothed the limb, gave it a winter grin.

Each day he sought the cream's restoring grace,
Till healed flesh took its long-lost, rightful place.
No scar remained, no infection in sight
Just grateful awe beneath the morning light.

"So dire a flame you quenched with hands of fire;
It fled like blaze that meets a cooling pyre.
What coin could pay the life you helped reset?
Name now your due, no sum will I regret."

"Just sixty yuan," Ray's gentle voice replied;
The youth stood still, his soul with wonder cried:
"So small a fee for all your cream and art!,
Have I not burdened both your skill and heart?"

"It suffices;" said Ray, "this sum is right.
Your joy alone will light my heart's dark night."
He smiled, and thanked that none named greed aloud;
For honor shone far more than gold endowed.

The young man, paid, passed by the neighbor's house,
Where sour words had crept out like some foul grouse:
"So cured at last from burns that ran so deep?"
"Yes, hail to Ray! My thanks I'll always keep."

At hearing Ray's rare charge, she called it greed,
"He rakes from all of us with grasping speed.
First thirty yuan, now sixty coins of gold,
Just in two moons!" Her bitter grudge took hold.

"What venom flows?" he cried, his face gone dark;
"Don't paint me with your thankless, hostile mark!
This life I owe, this new leg Ray did save!
Nor cast his name to your ungrateful grave!

"You moan of cost, complain of every pence?
His herbs outprice the sum of all your sense!
Did you pay for his labor or his art?
Or stab the hands that healed your broken part?"

"Sweet words for him! What bribes bought your defense?
His creams weighed naught, demanded no expense!"
"A bucket full of dung reeks with its stench;
Would you eat filth to fill a starving trench?"

"How dare you speak that way to age's ear?"
"Your spite compelled my speech; now let it clear!
That day red iron burned deep through my skin,
Ten tubes, eight score, but didn't soothe or win.

"My burns raged on, no ointment brought me rest;
The pain surged on, the fire of hell progressed.
For Ray's real cure? Sixty's a gift, not fee!
Six hundred yuan? Still just to set me free!"

"So filthy rich!" She slammed the door in heat.
"Not wealth!" he cried, "but justice fair and sweet!
It's virtue, debt, the conscience in your breast!"
Then silence spoke; her shame remained unpressed.

Each day brought those in pain so sharp and deep:
A woman's tongue had swelled beyond her lip.
Her mouth a cage, a prison dark and grim;
No food, nor drink, nor word could cross its brim.

He took his lamp to cast a steady beam,
Through shadowed paths to calm her strangled scream.
He plucked wild herbs where moonlit roadsides grew,
And crushed them all to yield their healing true.

Drop by slow drop, the spoon pried jaw apart;
The juice sank in, hope stirred her quiet heart.
By dawn she ate; by dusk, her health was whole,
Life taken back from death's oppressive toll.

No sooner home than urgency knocked loud:
A young man choked by urine's stifling cloud.

Ray knew the threat, the death's hourglass ran thin;
With lamp in hand, he sought fresh plants to win.

Banana roots he dug from sleeping land,
Then crushed to paste with salt's reviving hand.
He spread it thick where streams of life were bound;
In five brief minutes, freedom flow was found.

"Ray is Half-God, Miracle, Star-lit Grace;"
Such titles given for the lives he saved apace.
Their thanks confessed what skill and heart had wrought:
True healer's art with steadfast morals fought.

He placed all patients first, his meals forgot,
Through sleepless nights their urgent battles brought.
No pause, no rest, while suffering held command,
His life poured forth for every soul in hand.

Three decades passed; the mother-in-law gone;
Ray's first burn patient woke to guilt at dawn.
Though late, her heart with silent sorrow fell,
For unpaid debts no time could ever quell.

She kept a store where hardware goods were sold;
Her coffers full, yet inner peace grew cold.
The weight of words she never spoke aloud
Pressed down her soul beneath remorse's shroud.

Each morn she washed her face, still fair, unmarred;
Her gaze met eyes where silent tears stood guard.
"Just thirty yuan!" she whispered soft and low,
While tears traced the cheeks in graceful flow.

By day, the world cast care and grief aside;
By night, she dreamed of kin and endless pride.
She faced the ghosts that lurked within the dark:
Why spared your soul from thanks' neglected spark?

One night she saw Ray on the mountains high
Collecting herbs beneath a starlit sky.
The herbs that kept all fearsome scars afar
Would heal her wounds beneath the pale moon's star.

She ran to him, her eyes with glowing flame,
And cried, "Dear Uncle Ray, I bear the shame!
My mother-in-law 'n' I were weak, not strong;
We treated you unjustly—mean and wrong.

"I know we never paid the debt we owed
For roots and leaves that healed me on that road.
Your kindness poured like rain on barren sand,
Yet we returned with nothing in our hand."

He raised his hands to wipe her flowing eyes,
And smiled, "Release your grief; no more goodbyes."
That slight? A pebble tossed into the sea;
Forgotten all, and owe no debt to me.

"I rejoiced more than you when you were healed:
No mark endured where the harsh pain was sealed.
Your joy outshone the sun's resplendent light;
It filled my soul and set my spirit bright.

"So kind!" she breathed, her sorrow turned to dew.
He grinned and spoke sincere words sounding true.
"When you rejoice, my soul finds its own cheer;
Your peace becomes the tune I hold most dear.

"Abandon night, embrace the shining sun;
Walk free in bliss, your journey has begun!"
She nodded, cleansed by mercy's flowing stream;
Forgiveness wove her heart into a dream.

She woke at dawn, her former fears unmade;
A woman bathed in light, not sorrow's shade.
The dream had sown pure joy where pain had thrived;
New hope arose, her spirit was revived.

Favors Forever[13]

Toads' croaks rang loud along the country road;
She watched the sun ignite the morning's gold.
Beholding a troop pacing near her land,
She clutched her staff, each gesture firm and grand.

A small crowd gathered where the dust paths crossed;
Peace long had held the village, fear then tossed.
No thieves nearby, her door stayed open wide,
For son and grandson who bore food inside.

Like stormy skies, her mind with questions held;
Each footfall slow, yet measured and compelled.
She neared the door, a question, sharp as thorn:
Should I now shut what grief might leave forlorn?

"Grand-aunt!" A youth approached her door's domain;
As others followed fast in friendship's train.

---

[13] Note: This poem is adapted from a true account of good needs done by HUANG Huiying (黃惠英) of Jieyang, China.

Her cataracts veiled sight, and ears grown weak,
Yet their presence, no cause to make her bleak.

She swung her heart wide open, warm and free;
Then counted five where gathered joy would be.
"Hi, Aunt Veda," there came a voice she'd heard;
"Oh, come inside!" she called, though no name stirred.

For middle-aged, "Aunt Veda" rang with grace,
Yet peers would call her "Sister" with embrace.
The children's chant their loving link conveyed;
"You are?" she asked the dame in shadows' shade.

"I am Suna," warm tears upon her cheek;
"Have I been lost in memory so weak?
These gifts for you!" Down sorrow's pathways flowed;
Veda, distressed, saw burdens in that load.

"Why bring me gifts? Your presence gladdens me;
All gifts cost coin, such treasures are ne'er free.
But Suna, sit! Drink tea! Let no hearts ache;
Be here at ease, for friendship's gentle sake."

They took their seats around tea-table's span;
The steaming cups released a fragrant fan.
'Twas welcome brew for stories yet untold
More than the sip, their spirits it consoled.

Soft fragrant air of magnolias sent,
Caressed each happy face where'er it went.
It danced along where silence lay in deep;
Their thoughts like streams, unbroken, vast, and steep.

Veda poured first, hot streams from kettle's spout;
To warm the clay pot small as fruit held out.
Then quickly doused in careful, measured grace
The tiny cups in fine and shining space.

Next, tea leaves filled the pot's dark, waiting core;
They soon awoke beneath the steaming pour.
"This first wash flows like greens rinsed clean," some sighed,
But younger son claimed that with eager pride.

"Give me this brew, the finest, purest start!
Why waste what heaven crafts with patient art?
"High water, low tea": kettle held on high,
Four inches up, to stir leaves where they lie.

The server would then pour from spout kept low;
To tiny cups, three or five in a row.
"My turn," Suna's son offered, hands held sure;
Youths serve the old with customs rich and pure.

Then others rose, with gifts in careful hold:
They laid on tables fine treats rarely sold.

One pound per box, they shone in cheerful light,
Each morsel glinting in the room's warm sight.

"But why bring gifts?" Veda asked, half dismayed;
She eyed the spread generous hands had made.
"I merit none, nor will I take this store,
Yet thank your kindness to my humble door.

"Please take all back, let young ones eat the sweet!
The cookies will charm them when they retreat."
She moved to pack the bags with swift command,
As if by law all presents were straight banned.

"You are unchanged, whene'er I bear these things!
Yet your refusals bite with stings, stings, stings!"
Her tears then broke; her voice rang sharp and clear,
"You pierce my heart, this truth I hold most dear!

"My heart's torn should you toss what love intends;
Though humble, still for you this gift extends.
Whatever you say, all our gifts will stay;
They come with love, and so they mustn't stray.

"We traveled far to bring these gifts with care:
A token small for debts beyond compare.
They shall remain, though you may groan or plead;
With hearts sincere, we sow this lasting seed."

Her words drew forth the flood of tender cries,
Till long-held grief broke from her gentle eyes.
"But why, Suna?" her gentle voice addressed;
"I gave no deed deserving such a quest."

"You gave me nothing?" Suna's voice took flight,
"You shone through night and filled my soul with light!
This humble gift recalls love buried deep:
Fifty long years my soul was sworn to keep.

"To spurn these gifts would pierce my soul," she sobbed;
"Now peace, dear," Veda said, though heart still throbbed.
She could not grasp, yet Suna spoke and told
Of seventies' harsh famine, biting cold.

"Though hunger struck, your efforts eased our pain;
You gave me coins to buy life's golden grain.
Your daughters' needle-wealth made love expand;
Small change that fed the mouths your kindness planned.

"That year of death, when famine struck our land,
Your gifts fell sweet, as manna from God's hand.
Without your grace, my bloodline might've deceased;
This debt of life has never been released.

"I taught my young your mercy's honored tale,
Who stand today, through history's winding vale.

They come to honor love we can't forget,
The hands that spared us from the clutch of debt.

"Suna, 'twas five decades flown," Veda sighed;
"All counted, only coins; no debt should bide.
I blush to speak, though joy has filled my soul,
To see life thrive for every hungry whole.

"Yet still I grieve; I wished to give you more."
"But you had little; we all knew your store!
The grain you spared supplied the elders' need;
Your porridge thinned, you bore the famine's meed.

"I knew your sacrifice when gifts I gave,
You brushed aside what I had sought to save.
I stepped away, while grief weighed on my breast;
Today with kin I mend your kind behest.

"These gifts you must accept; we will not go,
Until you take the love our hearts bestow.
No treasures, only gifts sincere and true:
Some sweets, some tea, plain foods for children's view.

"I thought of gold, but knew it would depart;
Thus came these gifts, all offered from the heart."
"Oh, no! Not even sweets!" Veda declined;
"My tongue grows old, such treats I cannot find.

"Take back the sweets for children's joyful treat;
The tea is yours, a gift so rare and sweet.
Your love gleams dear; all goods demand their fee;
No gifts I need, yet happy I will be!"

Knock! knock! All heads turned toward the dull sound;
A figure stood upon the village ground.
'Twas Loyal Lad, with weathered, kindly face,
Who had borne gifts to grace her quiet space.

"Come in!" she called. "The door stands open wide!"
He entered, arms outstretched in warming tide.
He drew her close; her voice was stirred with joy:
"How wonderful it is to see you, boy!"

"This gift, dear Aunt," he said, "I bring for thee;"
Her eyes explored the bag like buzzing bee.
Within, fine foods and sweets! "But why such cost?
I'm glad you came, yet gifts have left me tossed!

"All things cost coin, what we buy, what we own;
I take no gifts; my heart shall not condone."
She spoke with care, "I need no rich display
Save your sweet smile that brightens my dim day."

"But Aunt," he said, "life's changed since long ago;
The fear of hunger is a bygone woe.

We have our fill of food, of cloth, of rest;
This humble gift reflects your noble zest.

"I know not what you mean," she softly said,
"Nor what great deed deserves this costly spread."
Then Loyal Lad recalled with heart renewed
One act of grace in gratitude imbued.

"That chill spring day," he said and met her grace,
"I toiled the field while rain fell swift apace.
No cloak to shield me, soaked right to the core;
So chilled and starving, turned homeward with sore.

"But trembling seized me fierce beyond control,
Near your bright hearth, despair had gripped my soul.
I saw you there; the porridge gently steamed;
You beckoned me; your warmth like sunlight beamed.

"Come wait the rain!" you said; I stepped in damp,
My limbs still shook beneath the fire's soft lamp.
"May I," I asked, "have just one bowl to eat?"
"Of course!" you said; "Forgive my lapse—take seat!"

You gave the bowl; my hunger quickly fled;
The chill withdrew; my spirit found warmth shed.
Yet shame burned deep as I did beg that day;
I told my mother how I'd lost my way.

"She soothed, 'Grieve not! Aunt Veda's soul is gold;
Her kindness overflows, so feel consoled.
She cares not for the treasures from her hold;
Her heart's a boundless, selfless, giving fold.'"

His eyes brimmed full; he'd prefer not to speak
Of the past shame, as he felt worn and weak.
Yet reason absent, gifts'd be cast aside;
Thus pride and love in silent war now vied.

She bade him pause: "Sit here, and let me hear
The tale of your success, of every year!"
Then said, "Take tea!" But Loyal Lad still pressed:
"You must accept the gift; let doubt find rest!"

"All right, all right!" she smiled and took the gift;
"I will, your grace gives my heart such a lift!"
First time she e'er took gifts without a fight;
This stunned sweet Suna in the bright daylight.

"Now look, Aunt Veda, surely that's unfair!
Why take his gifts and leave mine in despair?"
Veda prepared to calm Suna, but then
A strange car stopped before her home again.

A group appeared, led by a bent-back dame;
"My Sister Veda!" cried the dame by name.

"Oh, dear!" breathed Veda; then without delay,
The guest, supported by her son, made way.

She clasped her close; her arms held Veda tight,
A neighbor from the village's vanished night.
In native hamlet, wives from foreign lands
Were called by husbands' names through custom's hands.

Yet village-born held names like those above:
"Sister," "Aunt," or "Grand-aunt," that fit like glove.
"You are Do—?" said Veda, voice soft and low,
And paused to hear the name she used to know.

"Old neighbor Donna, dear!" returned the cry;
Then Donna faced the crowd of kin nearby.
She scanned the young ones clustered at the door,
And lifted voice as if to shake the floor.

"Now greet your Grand-aunt Veda!" Clear and strong,
They sang in praise, a chorus firm and long.
"Come in!" to youths outside, she gently spoke,
To couples, children—everyone awoke.

Each bore their bags with gifts prepared to stay;
They laid them on the table without delay.
"These gifts for you!" said Donna, pointing near,
Yet Veda frowned at all the joyful cheer.

She found fine teas and fresh sweets rich and dear,
Along with treats meant for close kin each year.
"Why so much?" Veda asked, perplexed in mind,
No memory of kindness left behind.

Fifty years past, when Donna's life was bare,
Like all, she had known hardship and despair.
"I'm glad you came, yet gifts I must decline;
All cost dear coin, and none here would be mine!"

"My son runs shops; he sent this tea for free;"
She said, "No coin was spent; it costs not thee!"
"But Donna, I drink water fresh and clear;"
The guest grew tense and shed a quiet fear.

Her son had come this very special day,
With loving gifts no time nor miles could sway.
She knew the years when hunger ruled the day,
Veda gave coins and food without delay.

She aided elders left with little care,
And neighbors trapped within despair's harsh snare.
In past, when Donna tried to give her pay,
Veda returned them all and ran away.

They knew her will, like iron, stood unbent;
Once fixed, no plea could shift her strong intent.

"This tea costs naught," Donna then pled her case;
"No purchase made; it holds no market trace."

"Your visit warms." Veda's strong will took part;
"But take all back; you've blessed my aging heart!
Now sit, be welcome! Let the stories start!
How fared your kin through years we lived apart?

"Four decades passed?" "Indeed!" arose the cries;
The past returned beneath time's vaulted skies.
Veda had left the village long before,
To bustling towns, then cities' crowded shore.

She tried young son's life on Toronto's land,
In Paris also, guided by fate's hand.
But home called loud; she chose the village lane;
Through years, Donna's life broke want's binding chain.

Her children left the plough for trade's bright road;
Each built four-storied wealth, a stately abode.
Grandchildren thrived with people of their own,
A harvest grown from seeds her grace had sown.

"My Sister Veda!" Donna's tears burst free,
Surprising host and guests with grief's raw sea.
Veda knew not the cause, yet held her peace,
Let silence reign till pain found its release.

"I've held these thanks through fifty years or more,"
She spoke from depths of her most grateful core.
Veda exhaled: no shadow seemed to loom;
Then stillness settled in the sunlit room.

"Well, Donna?" Veda asked, perplexed, concerned.
"Recall the days we had no hot meals earned?
Your burnt house' space you freely gave that day,
To let straw stove, our hungering souls, stay!

"Don't speak of that," Veda waved off the thought;
"The joy was mine to share what ruin wrought."
Though recent memory dimmed like faint stars,
The past stood clear, unbound by time's old bars.

Two houses left by mother, side by side,
Rented for just two dimes, the tenants tied.
Till fire claimed one, by chimney's wrathful spark,
Leaving but walls of clay and sand so dark.

Limestone and red hill clay stood bare and stark;
No roof remained, and no room left a mark.
She knew the tenant had no means to mend;
No suit she filed, no quarrel to defend.

No question asked if they'd repair the place;
No blame was laid, though ash defaced the space.

A bare shell 'twas where none could dwell or stay,
Yet Veda's grace forgave that fatal day.

The neighbor occupied the ground in sight,
Made roofless ruin serve the fowl's new right.
Half-floor became a coop where chickens tread.
While Donna's five kids cried for room to spread.

The house is small, four yards wide, seven deep,
Where parents' bed claims half the floor in keep.
A table stands, the stove takes room besides,
No space remains where children's hope resides.

So Donna placed her stove within the nook,
Where chickens ran and pecked, and stole each look.
The coop-man raged: "This filth-strewn, fowl-strewn ground,
No place for food where dirt and fowl abound!

"My birds roam free; your fire fills them with fright!
No cleanliness here meets a cook's clear sight!"
She knew the truth; she had no choice of place,
Yet feared to cook where fowl had left disgrace.

When talk with neighbor could not win the right,
She sought sweet Veda, heart of golden light.
"May I use but one corner?" low she laid.
Veda replied, "Yes!" lending gentle aid.

She spoke to coop-man: "Let Donna stay, cook."
He bowed to grace no petty strife could brook.
Then plastic sheet, stretched high by careful spouse,
Made roof for stove that used to cramp their house.

For years the stove gave warmth through rain and sun,
A kitchen rose where acts of grace begun.
Long lost to mind, that act of neighbor's grace,
A single leaf in kindness' endless space.

When all were poor, though coins for her ran thin,
She still spared dimes to help young hope begin.
At times gave rice, potatoes' earthy store;
As youth, bore water to a senior's door.

The burden weighed on her own household's need,
Yet pride she took in every selfless deed.
"I'm glad I helped through dark days' heavy tide;
At last she knew why she had made the ride.

"But gifts so rich? I must refuse them all!
Take back all teas and treats from this jammed hall.
"I live alone, eat little, crave no sweet;
I drink no brew, need naught but rice and meat.

"Your young ones home will treasure every bite;
Let joy bloom there in feasts and warm delight!"

Then Donna held Veda tight, swift and bold,
Her kin hid tea and cakes in cool nook's hold.

Veda fought hard to send the gifts away,
But Donna's strength soon broke her weak dismay.
Then like light, Donna flew through open door,
And left poor Veda helpless on the floor.

A sadness struck; how age had clipped her wing;
"Bye!" Donna cried, with joy that gifts would cling.
"Bye," Veda sighed, her voice a soft retort,
As love's forced bounty settled in her court.

When Veda turned, no soul was left in sight;
The first group had vanished in bright sunlight.
Loyal Lad too had gone, just gifts appeared,
All stacked where gratitude and awe adhered.

Though not her wish to keep what they had brought,
She bowed to loss in all the fights she fought.
"Why send such wealth?" she murmured to the air;
"Just come, no gifts! The cost is laid out bare.

"Each brand-name tea, each cake, each golden display
Bears hidden price that tales cannot convey."
None heard; their cheers rolled swiftly down the lane,
While all the gifts defied her soft refrain.

They praised their luck that timing gave the chance
To leave their love in one collective dance.
What fortune's grace! What smiling fate aligned!
To honor her where moon and sun combined!

Bare Bravery

A bleak mid-winter Monday held its clasp;
Sherlyn, a single mother, faced death's rasp.
An acid pain attacked within her chest,
As dawn's cold light broke winter's frozen rest.

She clutched the table, gasping anguished breath;
She dialed for help and cheated certain death.
"I'm dying—help! This torment will not cease;"
The agent sought her name and urged her peace.

Sherlyn wept that her girl, twelve, could not cope,
Her feeble mother lost all will and hope!
She moaned they'd drown alone; then silence fell,
When darkness took her, tolling time's lost knell.

She woke to strangers crowding by her bed:
White coats, blue uniforms, and silent dread.
The doctor'd repaired rupture in her heart
That spilled lifeblood and could have stopped their part.

A slight mishap would lead her to the grave;
She thanked the surgeon for his timely save.

While hospital wires tracked her heart's weak strain,
She heard an officer kindly explain.

"There is a program nearby run by state,
Where needy children may improve their fate.
Through pandemic's strain, now it gives free care:
Warm beds, full meals, and pastimes, all to share.

"Say yes, she'll stay until your health restores,
Then home, returned when public welfare roars."
The doctor added, "Surgery went well;
In a few days, home's bells will ring and swell."

Trust bloomed; she signed the forms with trembling hand:
Let CAS[14] now take her child, a fate so grand.
Though anxious, she was touched; relief's soft cry:
How grand to live in Canada; clear sky.

Five years of state support had freely flowed;
That helped release the burden of her load.
The rent was scaled to what her welfare brought;
The child support fulfilled what she had sought.

Indeed that was soft life without a thorn:
Now government would guard what she had borne!

---

[14] CAS is pronounced as /kæs/ in this poem, though it may be pronounced as /si:/, /ei/, /es/.

She wept with grateful tears, like morning's dew,
For systems built to be so strong and true.

While thinking of the doctors' healing art,
A sudden wave of warm tears broke her heart.
"How blessed am I!" This city's gifts unfold:
Free schools, free clinics, food for young and old!

Two days passed, then from hospital she strode;
As heart repaired, blood vigorously flowed.
One week at home, no shadow seemed to creep,
Yet Finna's absence stirred her soul to weep.

Then came resolve: "I'll bring her home!" she swore,
As ex-husband claimed rights he'd lost before.
"Why no consult with me?" His grievance poured;
She called CAS, asked their credit be restored.

"I've been discharged!" she pledged. "Now health will bloom!
Return my child and end this needless gloom!"
CAS vowed to act, but brought no child that night.
She called and called; solution not in sight.

Then came the call that turned her blood to ice:
"We know not where she is, no more advice.
Your daughter told of parenting's dark strain;
We meet tomorrow to discuss her pain.

Next morning, two cold agents rang her door,
With questions posed to wound her to the core.
"Is there no kin in town you've ever known?
Beyond your child and mother, you're alone?"

They asked if she was Canadian-born;
She shook her head, and felt their stare and scorn.
They showed disdain for how her words were said;
Two forms appeared and filled her soul with dread.

Lone mom thought that they'd bring back daughter soon;
She even talked with them with a sweet tune.
"I thank you from my soul's most sacred part
For guarding my child when I lost my heart."

"'Tis but our job," they said with practiced art;
The two clerks looked professional and smart.
She waited, dawn to dusk, yet no word came;
She called again, her anxious calls were lame.

Then their clerk struck her numb: "Seek mental care;"
Her shock and fear took over anger's share.
At noon new horror struck: "Your child is ill;
Hospitalized!" Hope surged against her will!

"I'll find her, nurse her, and I'll bring her home!"
She raced with her ex-husband through dawn gloam.
To local wards she gave her child's health file;

The clerk searched records with a vacant smile.

"No patient here." The walls dissolved to air;
Her child was gone, none knew her anywhere.
Her frantic search became a long nightmare,
Where she felt stabbed by many a harsh stare.

Three days slipped by; two CAS clerks came once more;
They bore false words that cut her to the core.
A letter, forged in Finna's chosen name,
Contained vile claims to stoke a mother's shame.

"You struck and scorned me daily!" the note whined;
That painted love as monstrous and unkind.
"No games, no rest! Just lessons stern and long!
No friends, no touch, no fries, all right and wrong!"

She read and felt her heart would snap in two:
"These lies, damned lies!" Her room grew black and blue.
"Who wrote this slander?" Blood at fevered pitch!
She knew her child could not conceive such switch.

She was too honest and too kind to frame
A mother's love with venom and with blame.
"Did you forge this? Force-sign her, think it smart?"
They watched her rage and shot their poison dart.

"Are you unwell? Should doctors now appear?"
"You need their care; not me! What nightmare here!"
Then silence spread; then whispers, poison air;
Then wordless, they departed, cold and bare.

Next dawn, eight cruisers, and a fire truck's might
Came lining her street in the morning light.
She watched the many uniforms soon spread;
"They come for me!" Cold terror filled her head.

Her daughter's teacher warned: "Two kids they caught;
You should stand firm though fear has fiercely fought!
If their knock is soft, no warrant is near;
Then just keep door shut tight on lawless fear.

"If the police have one, loud bangs will sound;
They'll break the door to play their grim game round.
Don't speak inside! Step out where others stand;
Let neighbors, friends guard truth on freedom's land!"

Fear gripped her heart on this famed foreign shore,
When soft knocks whispered at her trembling door.
"Police!" they called. "Wait out!" her voice replied,
Then phoned her friends to be her shield and pride.

They came and formed a solid wall of might,
Joined other souls who stood within the light.

"Now come with us," the officer declared.
"What offence then? No crime has been prepared!"

"We're told you seek to end your vital thread."
"I want my death?" she cried. "Who claims this lie?"
"It is the Children's Aid," the police swore.
"False!" Sherlyn cried. "I fight to live one more!

"If I sought death, why seek the healing art?
Why beg for pills to mend my broken heart?
CAS stole my child; I battle for her grace!
Not death, but justice, stands in this same place!"

"This cares not for your child," the cop announced,
"But they just feared despair'd have your fate trounced.
Come talk with help; let counsel ease your load."
"No!" Sherlyn stood. "I walk no such dark road!

"I'll never quit this life! My will stands tall!"
Defiance rang against the building's wall.
The neighbors' stares held officers at bay;
No hand could touch her on the public way.

One elder cop approached with practiced grace,
His voice a balm to mask the coming chase.
"We know the minds that mend the frail and pale;
Their cures make failing breath grow strong and hale.

"Your wounds need care? Let wisdom be your guide;"
Cool-headed, Sherlyn stood with iron pride.
"I will not go, though I respect your role;"
She felt cold terror grip her shaken soul.

Would these men chain her will and make truth lie?
Her friend's grim ordeal burned within her eye.
"Swallow these pills, or lose your child for good!
No word, no touch, as parenthood's neck should!"

She broke and drank the doctors' draughts entire;
Two weeks she was a ghost of thought and fire.
Released, she crawled, her limbs like heavy lead,
Flung pills to trash, defying what they bred.

No madness here, just CAS's cruel prey:
A mother's rage, sharp as a sword by day.
At last, police and sirens left the street;
She stood alone, no solace, grim defeat.

A fragile win, or just a fleeting spark?
While darkness pooled against the coming dark.
In soothing tears she thought she should repay
The teacher's kindness with a gift straightway.

Fine chocolate for counsel sage and deep,
Which barred the door where madness stalked in sleep.

Her wise advice had kept her spirit strong,
Saved her from wards where sanity goes wrong.

Fear lingered still; she couldn't face her home,
So slept five months on friendship's borrowed foam.
Yet hardship deepened at the court's command;
She stood accused on CAS's damned demand.

"A child abuser!" struck her like a blow;
"I love her more than life!" her voice rang low.
It then roared out: "She's my star, pure and true.
She eats wholesome meals, wears clothes fine and new.

"Beyond her peers, no need has gone unmet,
For higher learning, ninety grand's been set.
Her father and I, though we both are gray,
Secured her future for a brighter day.

"We'd give our girl a school life full of ease;
Thus child support is for her knowledge keys.
That's not for spending, but for learning's throne."
CAS lawyers gasped at sums they had just known.

They pounced, "Why take state housing, live in 'slum'?
Why cheat the public purse? Your crimes have come!
Tax dodger! Unfit mother! Common thief!"
Their slander bloomed; crushed truth found no relief.

"CAS lawyers, trained in lies with vicious guile;
They shred the truth, ambushed their prey with smile.
They stabbed my name with every poisoned dart,
And mercilessly tore my soul apart.

"I grant my answers shifted when confined:
At first, I signed the forms, distressed in mind.
But only while confined to sickbed's call;
When later "No!" burst from that fragile thrall.

"The judge asked Yes or No; for 'Why,' no place;
That shameful, unjust ruling sealed my case.
They stretched that shift to paint my spirit weak:
A fractured mind too shattered thus to speak!

"When sobbing broke me, what did they decree?
'Behold! Her madness plain for all to see!'
Till all believed: unfit, unwell, unclean,
The vilest liar court had ever seen."

The judge decreed that CAS transgressed no law;
Her child's removal stood without a flaw.
This verdict struck Sherlyn a crushing blow;
Then bold CAS moved to deal a second woe.

Their next assault: 'Prove physical attack!
Show mental cruelty!' They'd hold her back.

She'd lose her child forever, banned and barred;
No more hugs, sight, the bond be scared and scarred.

Sherlyn sought CTV, CBC's aid;
All major media spurned her, betrayed.
Famed justice fighters elsewhere turned her down;
Dismissed her pleas while wearing false renown.

Then letters flew to lawmakers on high,
To social workers too; all passed her by.
She shouted CAS's cruelty each day,
But agony persisted, would not fray.

From other cases, truth she came to learn;
Three scenarios caused a child's return.
Both parents would necessities withhold;
Rights yielded; or violence not well controlled.

Thus Sherlyn charged to all who would attend:
"CAS broke this law! I dare them to defend.
No cause met, no just pretext to invade:
My daughter torn by their unlawful blade."

She armed with statutes, studied through the night,
Devoured the law till justice burned so bright.
Through CAS's maze, she honed her battle skill;
A mother's love turned fortress, strong and still.

She learned their pay: from eighty grand a base
To one-five-oh, all grasped with greedy grace.
Their funds increased by every captive head:
Each child a coin, from whom a dollar's bled.

"Six hundred charged per hour; steep lawyers' fee,
Nineteen thousand per month, the foster's key.
All feast on anguish, thriving on our pain;
Their gold flows where our murdered love is slain.

"They charge without a shred of proof or sign;
To steal my child, they'd fracture the divine.
But I hold papers scorching with the truth;
Their abuse stamped on every page, forsooth."

Two years of darkness, silent, wordless, dry,
No thread to trace where hidden child might lie.
What walls concealed her? What grim shadows fall?
Truth buried deep where justice builds its wall.

May's sun beamed bright, four months since hope's first spark,
But twenty-eight since darkness stole her lark.
"I'll visit, Mom!" a cheerful voice declared;
The call left Sherlyn stunned and unprepared.

Dawn found her buying fruit and cookies sweet;
Child's favorite food cooked, a loving treat.

At ten-twelve's triple knocks, Sherlyn screamed out;
She swung the door. "My child!" came forth her shout.

"Mom!" Girl flew into her long-waiting arms;
"My child!" Sobs shook her soul with love's alarms.
"Let me behold you more than dreams could hold!
Each day, each night, I've ached." "Me, too," sobs told.

Their bond by blood no force could break or bend;
A love no power on earth could ever end.
Mom raised child's chin: "You look so frail, my dear."
"I'm sick." A cough, then one and silent tear.

She wandered from the sofa, bed, then bath;
She staggered, strength had fled, dread marked her path.
Another harsh cough: crimson stained the air;
"Oh God!" Sherlyn screamed, clutching to a chair.

"To ER now! No second to delay!"
"Yes, Mom." They raced where white-coats hold their sway.
Ten minutes passed; the ER doctor spoke,
"Why wait so long?"—his tone a stinging stroke.

Then patient coughed fresh blood, convulsed in pain,
While Sherlyn braced for blame's corrosive rain.
"Delayed care means abuse I must report;
Police'll decide if you shall go to court."

"CAS caused this! Twenty-eight months' brutal power!
She came today; we rushed here through the hour!"
The doctor murmured: "CAS, again?" Then fast:
"To ICU! Let no test be bypassed!"

Labs showed thirteen flags: TSH at zero's state,
Thyroid flat-lined, life fading past night's gate.
Two years of hunger, cold, a cruel start
Had sapped her strength and broke her youthful heart.

Her health card seized by CAS's cruel hand,
Yet clerk restored its power with a command.
Staff fought with skill, through one month's tender care;
They mended bones and taught her feet to dare.

When well, they dared not seek home, dread in chest,
Lest CAS and cops attack at law's behest.
The predators would ambush mom and child;
This terror drove them to the cold, dark wild.

With help from friends and those by CAS once torn,
They rented a small bungalow, forlorn.
They settled somewhere no soul knew their name,
A hidden harbor from the grasp of shame.

While Finna lay in guarded mental care,
Sherlyn struck truths at powers throned in air.

MPPs, ministers, and Premier heard
Her facts tear lies, demand justice's word!

Her words stirred action; now, aligned, awake;
That fall, the province moved for justice' sake.
It launched long-stalled inquest toward their case,
That deep dark place's reckoning to face.

Now safe in walls, where no dark knock invades,
Mother and child wept joy: no more charades.
They'd never part! Together live, they swore;
Together die, one heart forevermore!

With daughter clutched, mom's gentle question fell:
"Who forged that lie, that sent our bond to hell?
That letter! I know you: you'd never maim
Your mom with wounds, with words of torture's claim."

"Mom—!" Finna wept, hysteric, bruised, and torn:
"They threatened, forced me, left me silence-sworn!"
Sherlyn held daughter tight, love's shield unfurled,
"You're safe now. Speak. Truth breaks the chains that curled."

"They threw me in a madhouse! Drugged my dawn:
Pills jammed down my throat, then strength ripped, withdrawn.
Mentally ill, addicts stalked the wretched hall;
I feared their bite, their scream, the madhouse thrall."

"A crime!" gasped Sherlyn ere the child replied;
"I asked them 'Why?' Their agents coldly lied.
'You'd kill yourself!' But I swear 'twas untrue!
They drugged me till my will dissolved like dew.

"They trap all kids this way, I pledge, I swear;
They dope them dumb so none can truth declare."
Sad Finna watched her mother's face ignite
With rage's fire no time could ever blight.

"Two weeks of drugs left weakness buried deep;
I shuffled steps, no strength to run or leap.
My muscles—gone!" Sherlyn's curse rent the air,
"God damn them! Why this vile, soul-crushing snare?"

"They moved me to a home two spouses shared,
A paired and truthful bond between them bared.
Though kind, their new union left me disgraced;
Three months, then back to CAS I was displaced.

"Then 'twas this home where two grown sons dwelt low;
Upstairs stood my room, but you'd hate to know.
They'd climb each night to guard my sleep, they spoke,
And sat upon my bed—her feigned calm broke.

She sobbed and wept, "Alone, afraid, undone;
I can't—don't ask—what darkness they have won.

They ruined me, that household's cruel art;
Now nightmares see my peace of mind depart.

Sherlyn held tight, "My child, you're safe with me;
You feel my arms, your fortress, strong and free!
No ghost shall touch you, no more fear or flight;
I stand your shield by day, your lamp by night!"

"At that madhouse, they made me write a lie:
'Confess she's bad!' A voice rose, thin and dry.
I said no first, but then came threats of war:
No phone 'n' Wi-Fi, food locked behind the door.

"They hissed: 'Your mom won't know; these words stay sealed!'
I froze. They flung slurs, slanders thus revealed.
I stalled; they scrawled it, thrust page in my hand;
My shaking pen obeyed their vile demand.

"I'm sorry!" But mom cried, "You're faultless, child!
That scrawl? I knew your heart: pure, undefiled.
When they showed it, I charged, 'Who penned this lie?'
Their utter silence screamed a coward's cry."

"Next day, CAS claimed: 'We'll guard your note secure;
Your mother died in sleep so deep and pure.
The doctors failed; could not save her,' they lied."
Sherlyn roared: "Damn washouts! Let them be tried!"

Her cheeks burned hot; her heart beat wild, uncontrolled:
For her, I'll calm rage, keep my child consoled.
She breathed: *Through dread, my health I must retain;*
For Finna, I shall shatter every chain.

To Sherlyn, CAS had stolen living gold:
Her daughter, now twelve, soon thirteen years old.
More rare than crowns of gems the world might hold,
'Twas life no wealth could purchase or enfold.

She read online of young girls trafficked cheap,
Kidnapped for sex or organs they would reap.
Before last sigh, their hearts still pulsed alive,
Were harvested so foul rich men would thrive.

Each teen "donated" through consent by lie:
Predators' forms make cruel laws comply.
Some captives starved in dungeons, starkly cried,
Tortured for organs until each one died.

Each organ fetched half-million-dollar breeze,
While victims died despite agonized pleas.
No duvet e'er bought, though thrift stores bestow,
Pure evil in a system's venal glow.

In shock she shivered: ten tubes left child's vein;
Blood tests drawn drained her spirit's fragile reign.

What purpose claimed such volume? Dark, unkind!
She dared not face the dread that roamed her mind.

She quelled suspicion, sighing low and deep,
"These don't occur where democracies weep.
We live in Canada, a moral land,
Where law and order firmly take their hand."

They shared their horrors till the sun arose;
Each thread revealed fresh agonies and woes.
Then, the mad wards where predators held sway:
Two weeks of torment broke all pride to stay.

Then, crimes concealed by lies of mother's death:
"She's gone forever," spoke the hated breath.
So no one left to mourn; no love to miss;
Save numb obedience in the dark abyss.

Yet Finna learned her pillar had survived,
And bought gold gifts for her as she contrived.
But CAS sent none out for her, low, unkind:
Another theft to scar her stolen find.

By their mean acts, Sherlyn perceived with fright,
They would just keep their prey confined, held tight.
All hope was razed as CAS trashed every note,
Defiled their blood bond, and its grandeur smote.

They blocked her calls, erased her name to spite,
And sought to kill the final kinship light.
As thieves and liars, slaves to their dark crime,
They dug innocence' grave before its time.

The child then told they fed her rotting bread:
Scraps saved from dreadful tricks on black mold's bed.
The heat was turned so low on winter's night;
At ten degrees, thin blanket failed the fight.

She shook with fever every day, health marred;
But cruel hands had stolen healthcare card.
Stone hearts barred her from each doctor and nurse;
For doom the demons lured the girl to curse.

Sick, weak, how many times she looked death-pale!
Sherlyn absorbed this vicious new-told tale.
"This plot," she gasped, "seeks live organs for pay?
To sell her parts, and leave her to decay?

"Why freeze her form? Block care? Here's terror's cry:
Death brings grand profit; in vile trade they vie.
Used quilts and coats cost coins, free clinics stand,
Yet their command enforces devil's brand."

Three months crept by; the province probed child deaths,
While CAS made its threat with menacing breaths.

"Return your child or jail will be your fate!"
Sherlyn stood firm: "I will not yield to hate!"

They pitched new poison: "Sign on this decree,
'She sickened in my care,' then she'll be free."
Outrageous! Sherlyn burned with righteous fire,
For dignity, she would quell their desire.

Still hid, they braced for handcuffs, court, and cell,
Two warriors in their covert, guarded shell.
Then sudden shift arrived, with pressure's weight;
CAS closed her case, no false confession's bait.

"Just keep this quiet," humble CAS now pled;
The truth yet roared where'er her footsteps led.
"No private vengeance guides what I disclose;
I fight to spare all parents equal woes."

O mother-lioness, your valor's vast!
Canada's highest honor should be cast.
Your courage shone throughout the long dark night;
You turned wronged love into unyielding light!

www.ingramcontent.com/pod-product-compliance
Lightning Source LLC
Chambersburg PA
CBHW022014160426
43197CB00007B/418

* 9 7 8 1 8 9 6 8 4 8 3 3 4 *